To Charlene —
With love and special prayers.
Helen Jean Parks
Ephesians 3

Holding the Ropes

Holding the Ropes

Helen Jean Parks

BROADMAN PRESS

Nashville, Tennessee

4251-94
ISBN: 0-8054-5194-3

This book is the text for a course in the subject area *Missions* of the Church Study Course.

Dewey Decimal Classification: 248.3
Subject heading: PRAYER

Library of Congress Catalog Card Number: 83-70004
Printed in the United States of America.

To Keith
With gratitude to God
for
surpassing my highest dreams and desires
when answering my prayer
for a life partner and friend

Boldly I Pray

So lead me
   that I might hear
      the cry of lostness
         and turn to give your name.
   To remember,
      that when you touched me
         with burning coals of your
         cleansing
            you sent me too.

Help me
   that as I pray with you
      I do not forget
         your great concern
            for this lost world
               as evidenced
                  by your Son,
            and,
               your sending him,
                  and his sending me.

Boldly!
   Then I pray
      (though with some trembling)
   Lead us
      to all the corners of the earth
         and to its people.
   Even
      at the cost
         of my going too.

—WENDELL BELEW

# Foreword

William Carey presented the first missionary to the newly-organized missionary society. He was Dr. Thomas, a young Christian surgeon who had gone out under the East India Company. Greatly impressed with the deep needs of lost people, he had returned to raise funds and seek a companion for going back.

"From Thomas's account," one of the men recalled, "we saw there was a gold mine in India, but it seemed almost as deep as the center of the earth. Who will venture to explore it?"

"'I will go down,' said Carey to his brethren, 'but remember that you must hold the ropes.' We solemnly engaged to do so; nor while we live, shall we desert him.'"[1]

Praying for and giving to missions has been likened to holding the ropes for missionaries who go. In Carey's day it was more dangerous and precarious, but it has never been easy to go.

The quest is not for mere gold, but for souls of persons, any one of whom is more valuable than the entire physical universe and far more precious to God.

Not included in these thoughts on prayer are some of the essential ingredients like praise, thanksgiving, and confession of sin. Much has been written of these in other books. I have dealt mainly with some prayer principles as related to missions or those about which less is written.

It would be impossible to read the multitude of books on prayer. but of the ones I scanned, it seemed striking that the great classics are centered on intercession that is evangelistic and missionary. They are not focused on prayer for self or even for others only at our doorsteps, but including others to the ends of the earth.

The kind of "holding" prayer the cause of missions requires is not passive or inactive.

When Christians put on every piece of our Christian armor, we are ready for the battle. Does Paul say, "Now *fight*"? No, he says, "Now *pray*." In the great prayer passage in Ephesians 6:13-18, the focus of our whole Christian experience is praying. It is the climax of our preparation for doing God's work.

We are outfitted, not for defense, but for offense. We are to storm the gates of hades. Jesus promised they could not stand against our onslaught. We are to assault Satan's strongholds and pull down every barrier he erects.

We are to take the world by praying, loving, and witnessing.

Giving his disciples the keys to the kingdom, Jesus told them they had power to bind and loosen on earth as it has already been willed in heaven.

Those of us who are his body on earth (the church or the called-out ones) are the ones through whom God carries out here what has been determined in heaven. We have the opportunity to be part of what he is doing.

I think he meant that we can help determine whether persons and nations are given or denied the chance to enter Christ's kingdom by whether we share or fail to share Jesus' gospel.

The God of the universe is offering us the greatest privilege afforded human beings, a chance to participate in his eternal purpose by praying, giving, and going. We can decline because of ignorance, refusal, or simple neglect.

In announcing Jesus' coming birth, the angel said, "He will save his people from their sins" (Matt. 1:21, RSV).[2] How unutterably tragic to miss knowing Jesus Christ as Savior!

Just as tragic for God, others, and ourselves is to miss the fact that he saved *us* from *our* sins to "prevent" *others* from "missing the end and scope of life," which is himself (Matt. 1:21, AMP).[3]

Contents

1
A Call to Prayer

Passing my nine-year-old daughter's bedroom one afternoon I saw her crying and thought something terrible had happened at school that day. Instead, she was consumed with something far more important. "If the journeyman dies," she wept, "there will be one less missionary."

For several days we had been praying each mealtime for Larry Hughes, a twenty-four-year-old missionary journeyman who had been seriously injured only five weeks into his two-year assignment. On an outing with young people, Larry had dived from an eight-foot rock into water only two feet deep.

Though his spinal column was not severed, he suffered three fractured and dislocated vertebrae, plus skull lacerations, and was having respiratory distress because of swelling. Fever compounded the seriousness of the accident.

Daily my husband brought progress reports of Larry's situation when he returned from work at the Foreign Mission Board's home office. We couldn't know all the crises and attendant miracles that were taking place, but we prayed.

That afternoon I sat down on the bed by Elóise and we prayed to the Lord to spare Larry's life and heal him, if that were his will. Shortly afterwards we heard he was in Dallas' Baylor hospital receiving treatment, still paralyzed and still fighting for his life.

Later we were to learn from a news release details of a miraculous thirty-eight-hour flight transferring Hughes to an American hospital better equipped to handle his case. In spite of a severe shortage of physicians, Malawi's president granted special permission for two of the nation's twenty doctors to accompany the patient.

As the British Overseas Airways plane approached London's airport, the tower reported heavy fog had descended and the ceiling was below minimum. The pilot was advised to divert to Scotland. This would have meant a long overland trip returning Hughes to London, and a significant delay in transferring him to a trans-Atlantic flight.

"'I'll give it five more minutes,' the BOAC captain informed missionary Roy G. Davidson, Jr., traveling with Hughes' party. 'But there isn't much chance the fog will lift. It is dropping, not rising.'

"Davidson testified to the miracle. 'As we were on the final approach, the fog rose to the minimum 900 meters with 200 meters visibility. No one in the plane or the tower could believe it. The minute we touched down, it dropped again and no more planes could land.'"[1]

I do not remember how much longer I continued to pray before becoming concerned with other matters. In fact, I had largely forgotten the incident two years later when, at a Foreign Missions assembly, returning journeymen convening for debriefing were recognized. Special mention was made of Larry Hughes who stood on crutches to a thunderous applause.

When I met him afterwards, I told him of the experience with my daughter. "I want to meet her!" he exclaimed. Later as she approached him to introduce herself I happened to be standing at a distance. Tears blurred the scene for me.

The experience with my daughter was an emotional one from beginning to end. But I really don't think emotions had anything to do with God's answer. Others were praying who probably did not "feel" the emotions we did.

Prayer must rest on something far more stable than our own emotions. It is grounded in God's character, his Word, and his will. Our response springs not from emotion but from obedience—an act of our will.

Most of us wait to pray until we feel like it. Maybe that is why we pray so little.

Another reason we pray so little is that our outlook, even as Christians, is far more secular than we realize.

12

The story of Larry Hughes and others like it challenge our usu way of seeing and living in the world. We talk about prayer. We open and close services with prayer. And sometimes we pray. But when we do, we are going against our independent human nature. Our society and often our churches see prayer as the least valuable and effective thing we do.

This book has been written to encourage you in prayer. Don't wait until you finish reading the book to pray. When some biblical insight or truth speaks to you, put the book down and let this truth become a part of your conversation with God.

Where a story of answered prayer inspires you, use this as an invitation to prayer. Personal, even selfish, concerns may distract you from concentrating on either reading or praying. Stop and tell God every detail of what is bothering you.

Nothing need keep us from praying. Everything that happens to us can be a stepping-stone to prayer.

Don't wait until you feel like praying.

"When my heart doesn't feel like praying," explains missionary Ida Davis, "I go ahead and begin with my mind anyway, knowing the Lord takes what I give him and goes on from there, leading me up and out gradually, if not dramatically."

Missionary Barbara Vick "realizes more and more I am 'getting through' even when I don't have an emotional experience while praying."

One of the greatest pray-ers and missionaries ever, Hudson Taylor was asked if he ever prayed without any consciousness of joy. "Often," was his reply. "Sometimes I pray on with my heart feeling like wood. Often, too, the most wonderful answers have come when prayer has been a real effort of faith without any joy whatever."

But real feelings can be a real part of praying. In fact, they can make your praying real. Look at the psalmist's prayers. He expresses anger, jealousy, depression, rejection, blame, doubt, and other "non-Christian" emotions.

Many Christians think we can only talk about certain things to

pray only the kinds of prayers we hear in public
onder we quit praying!

ns view feelings and desires as things to be put aside
as we grow spiritually. Ralph Herring counseled
eally wanted to pray to make the most of their
and desires.

"Begin where you are rather than where you think you ought to be, I say. Ask God for the things you want. Even if what you want is something as childish as a little red wagon (or a big shiny automobile) brighter than any other kid's in the neighborhood—if you *really* want it, ask him for it! Voicing desires that are real to you will put zest into your asking. And you are in a better position to be dealt with by God on that plane (low as it may be) than on the plane which you pretend to want (which is even lower). The child can grow; but the hypocrite, confined in his shell of sophistication, cannot. Ask for what you *want*. Begin *there*, God does."[2]

In the beginning you may have to take yourself in hand, sit yourself down, and pray. It may seem like a burden or duty at the beginning. But from God's side, it's not either a burden or a duty that he's laying on you. God loves you whether you come to him in prayer or not. He loves you when you come with a cold or angry heart. He loves you even when you are more concerned about building your own kingdom rather than his. If we had just a small glimpse of how much God loves us and wants to bless us, we would rush to our prayer time each day.

Another factor that we seldom think of is what prayer means to God. "We are slow to see the fiercely burning passion of God's heart in respect to men. We see prayer as for our benefit only. What God wants to do through prayer too often eludes us entirely. The picture changes when we think of prayer in terms of what it means to him. Under the limitations he has voluntarily assumed by dealing with man as a free agent, his intense yearnings for men seem all but shut up to this one means of fulfillment. His heart's desire can be laden on nothing except upon our own desires. The strength and intensity of our concern measure our capacity for his. Our longings reveal our affinity to him."[3]

14

So come to him. Let him love you. Let his love transform you. Let his love flow through you to people who are separated from God and who haven't heard how much he has done to bring them back home.

2
Prayer Partners

It works! my heart cried. It works! Prayer works!
I knew the elation of a wonderful answer to prayer.
No, checked my mind. *God* works! Not prayer!
To say "prayer works" or to talk about "unleashing the power in prayer" makes it inanimate and divorces it from God.

It is like Stewart Newman's small son saying, "Daddy, did you know God doesn't make it rain? Clouds do!" In his young mind it had to be *either* God *or* clouds. It could not be *both and*.

Splitting hairs perhaps, but I resist any impression given that "clouds of prayer" are what produce rains of blessing. Without God there would be no rain or miracles (or clouds or prayer either, for that matter). God has ordained clouds to make it rain. God has ordained us as partners to redeem his world. He has entrusted us with prayer to make it happen.

Through prayer God creates responsiveness.
Missionary James Young dreaded his Thursday trips to a remote, inland village that was difficult to reach and unresponsive. It was his hardest trip of the week. He was tiring of the seemingly fruitless visits, he told his wife Gwen.

Then one Thursday it changed! Thirty-two adults said they wanted to believe in Jesus. Twenty relatives in a neighboring village responded also.

A few days later a letter came from Emmett Dunnevant in Glen Allen, Virginia, saying he had begun praying for the Youngs every Thursday on a regular basis.

15

Through prayer God delivers from death.

About ten years ago the Gilbert Nichols family was involved in a very serious traffic accident. Most critically hurt was Becky, sixteen, their oldest daughter, with multiple injuries, including a broken arm and leg, severed ear, and broken jaw. She was losing blood quickly.

"The Lord took care of us," declared her mother, Deane, explaining how Becky was taken in a miraculous way to the Baptist hospital instead of to a first-aid station where they were not prepared to treat such injuries.

The day before the accident a Paraguayan man had appeared at the hospital wanting to give blood. "That in itself is unusual," explained Deane. "People here seldom donate blood willingly, even for their own families." Because he had a rare blood type, the lab technician declined. Taking his name and address, they promised to call if they needed that type later.

Returning a second time, the man insisted on donating his blood. To keep from insulting him, the technicians took it. The next day when Becky was brought to the hospital, she had lost so much blood she had no blood pressure. Her blood type was the same as the insistent donor's! It was immediately available!

Missionary ham operators contacted families in the United States. Judy Lowman, Baptist Woman's Missionary Union director in Deane's home church in Cabot, Arkansas, heard the news and checked the time. At the exact moment of their accident, she had been praying for them. While dusting her dining room, she had moved the lace doily they had given her on furlough. Other times she had done it without thinking. Today she had been impressed to stop and pray.

Later it looked as though Becky would lose her arm because of infection. When the doctor warned he might not be able to save it, she thought of all the years she had practiced piano with the goal of being a pianist. Telegrams, letters, and calls assured the family of prayers. The arm began to heal.

Eight months later Becky left on crutches, returning to college in the United States. Having worked as a missionary journeyman, she and her husband, James A. Smith, are now serving as career missionaries in Europe.

Through prayer God opens "prison" doors.

"While I was Missionary-of-the-Week and you were praying for me, I had a most unusual experience," relates Amelio Giannetta.

He received a special permit to visit Nancy, a young Chinese convict imprisoned four years previously for smuggling fifty pounds of heroin.

Announced over the prison's loudspeaker as the ambassador, he marveled, "I do not know where the guards got that idea, but they were not far wrong. Indeed I was Christ's ambassador."

Guards watched his slightest move as he talked with the girl two hours in a private audience room. At the conclusion, a smile lighted her tearstained face as she gave her heart to Jesus.

Preparing to return to her cell, she asked what day it was. "I must remember this day," she explained, "I am more free now inside these walls than I was in the outside world!" "She had indeed obtained freedom in Christ," affirmed Giannetta.

Through prayer, God reclaims a preacher for his people.

"Since Michael Duis is the only seminary graduate from the Kadazan people, the region's largest ethnic group," missionary Charles H. Morris relates, "we had been counting on his returning to spearhead a program for reaching them." Instead, he quit the ministry in July.

Efforts for several months to reenlist him proved futile. Discouraged and under family pressure, he had shunned all meetings with Chuck or others.

"On January 13 I felt I should try one more time to find and talk to him. The next day I started out with a fellow pastor, not knowing where we were going. We met a Kadazan woman who took us up the trail toward the mountain where he lived. We crossed four rivers, one of them on a swinging bridge, crawled through undergrowth, and finally came to his mountain after climbing upward for an hour.

"The woman told us to cross the river and climb the mountain. Halfway up, she advised, we should call. We followed instructions, crawling almost straight up, literally on hands and knees. At last we spotted a house in the jungle and called. No one answered.

"I thought we had failed again, when he finally appeared at the

17

door. Living alone in this lonely place, he made no move at first to welcome us. Eventually, though, he invited us to climb the stairs to his house.

"When I shared with him my mission, he seemed moved that I cared. But he was adamant against returning to the ministry. There were family problems and he felt rejected by his parents. After thirty minutes I suggested we pray. He agreed reluctantly. I poured out my heart to God on his behalf and then rose to leave. I felt dejected.

"'While you were praying,' he said, 'God spoke to me and I had a revelation. I am ready to go to work in February.' 'What work do you mean?' I asked. 'Whatever the Lord will let me do to reach my people,'" he responded.

The next morning Duis arrived at the Morrises' home, smiling and happy. Morris put him in touch with a church willing to sponsor him and also felt impressed to approach a Chinese businessman and longtime friend about providing part of Duis' expenses. He agreed readily.

The Morrises did not know that on January 13 about one hundred members of the First Baptist Church, St. Clair Shores, Michigan, prayed for them, more than nine thousand miles away. When they received short notes of encouragement from the pastor and church members on January 25, they learned of the special prayer time.

"It had all seemed so easy," Morris recalled. "Now I know why."

3
✐Prayer and God's Plan

Soldiers in combat need a larger picture of the fighting than just what they can see and hear from their isolated position. They may feel completely surrounded or hopelessly outflanked by the enemy. It is crucial that they be in contact with their own command post and get an overview of the whole battle.

When we become part of Christ's body, the church, we enter spiritual combat whether we know it or not. Joining Christ sets us against Satan, the present world system, and our own human nature. Prayer is a key part of our spiritual warfare. It is our link to our command post. Through prayer and God's Word we are able to see God's plan. Seeing it and understanding it give us courage in our battles and enable us to help other Christians in theirs.

God's plan began before the world was created. It will continue after the world has passed away. It is for his glory. It is for all persons and nations.

God created man and woman in his spiritual likeness to live and have fellowship with him forever. He gave them dominion over his world as a trust.

They doubted and disobeyed God, rejecting his rule over them because they wanted to be equal with him. As a result, they were faced with a state of spiritual death, pain, hardship, and eventually physical death. They cut themselves off from fellowship with him, destined to be separated in this life and forever.

They entered the spiritual warfare between God and Satan. By disobeying, man became an enemy of God, developed an aversion to him, and, by default, forfeited his God-given dominion of the world to Satan.

God set a plan in motion to bring back all men to himself. He first chose a man (Abraham), then a family (Jacob and his twelve sons), finally a nation (Israel), guiding, blessing, and revealing himself, so he could reach out to all other nations.

He promised Abraham he would bless him so he could be a blessing to all nations. As he broadened the scope of his plan to Jacob and then to the nation of Israel, he reaffirmed that his purpose and concern was for all nations.

All peoples of earth are God's, according to Dr. H. Cornell Goerner, but a special people was needed to serve as a holy priest nation, mediating between God and all other peoples, on the condition of obedience and keeping the Covenant.[1]

God entered his people into "spiritual kindergarten," teaching them basic truths, laws, and principles about himself and his plan of faith.

He used visual objects to show them spiritual truths. The Temple and its furnishings, animal sacrifices, and a system of offerings were designed to teach them how to approach and worship him. These symbols spoke to them about their need of forgiveness and redemption from sin, and about a life of prayer and fellowship with God.

He gave the Law, knowing it was impossible for them to do what it required. Its purpose was not to put them right with him but to make them aware of their sinfulness and his holiness.

He appointed priests, showing that persons must approach a holy God through a mediator by way of sacrifice. He insisted on purity in their lives as they drew near him. The animals they sacrificed were a symbolic substitute for their own death caused by sin.

Bit by bit and in many different ways God revealed himself and spoke to his people through the prophets about his plan, ways, and purposes for them.

Finally the exact time arrived for God to communicate perfectly with man. He spoke by means of THE WORD, Jesus Christ, his Son who came to embody and personalize his message.

Through his Son he had decided to bring the world back to himself by showing how much he loved us. While we were still sinners and his enemies, Christ became a human being, lived a perfect life, and substituted himself for us by dying on the cross.

He died and rose from the dead that we might be forgiven of sins and rescued from Satan's kingdom of darkness and death. It is by his death and resurrection that we receive a new quality of life now and live in union with God forever.

Knowing we cannot save ourselves, we accept by faith his sacrifice for us, turn from our own way of sin and self, ask for and receive his salvation. He gives us new life and brings us safely into his kingdom of light. We become his children.

He has provided us with every spiritual blessing possible, since we are his heirs. He wants us to experience his presence and fellowship, to share in all the promises he has given, and to receive every good thing we need to do his will.

Not only does he want us to know and enjoy him and receive his blessings, but he wants this for every person in the world.

God's great desire is that not one single person be destroyed by sin but that every person should turn back to him. The purpose of his coming, Jesus said, was to search for and save all persons lost.

Every time he saves anyone he expects that person to participate in his plan. "In the same way for the same purpose the Father sent me," Jesus declared, "I am sending you" (see John 20:21).

He gives us his blessings for a purpose: that we might share and pass them on.

God has made us ambassadors for Christ, entrusting us with the message of reconciliation. We are to proclaim Christ to everyone so that all may be brought into union with Christ.

Those of us who trust Christ are the spiritual children of Abraham, the "spiritual Jews," and God's chosen people. He has made us a nation or royal race of priests. We have been given the authority and responsibility to mediate between God and every other person in the world.

We are to offer petitions, prayers, requests, and thanksgivings to God for all people, because he wants them all to be saved.

The key to God's plan is Christ in you.

He is not just an *external* Savior, not just a Helper *alongside* us, but he actually, literally lives *within* us by his Spirit, living his life through us. The only hope of our becoming all he wants us to be and doing all he plans us to do is Christ living in us.

Just as we could not save ourselves, so we cannot live the Christian life. Through dying to ourselves, our own desires and conveniences each day, by faith, we ask him to live through us.

If we are crucified voluntarily every day, his mind can think through us, his love can love through us, his strength can work through us, his voice can speak through us, his life can live through

21

us, his prayers can be voiced through us.

The essence of God's plan is Christ.

Paul says God has a secret plan, now revealed, which he will carry out through Christ. It is to bring all creation together under the lordship and headship of Jesus Christ. The simplest summary of his plan is found in Ephesians, chapters 1 and 3, and Colossians 1:27-29. Each time Paul speaks of it, he intercedes for Christians that we can grasp God's plan and so become more willing and more effective co-workers with God.

As we enter into the salvation of God, as Christ is born within us and lives in us, we can't help but become a part of God's plan to bring his lost creation back to himself. The American Baptist theologian A. H. Strong grasped this in a beautiful way:

"The church is the expanded Christ, and the purpose of foreign missions is the purpose of the universe, to multiply Christ, to reincarnate the Son of God, to enthrone Christ in the hearts of men, to make all men the temples for his personal indwelling, that he may be the first-born among many brethren, and may fill the world with himself.

"But Christ multiplied himself through the self-multiplication of the individual Christian. He has kindled his light in our souls that we may give that light to others. How long it has taken us to realize that the command to "Go" is addressed not to official servants, but to all Christians, and that Christ's purpose is to make every convert a missionary! *Crescit eundo* is the motto of his army—it grows as it goes. Every enemy subdued is to become a recruiting officer, and the whole population is to be enlisted as his forces sweep on.

"Christian love begins at home, but it does not end at home. Like the circles set in motion when you throw a stone into calm water, it widens evermore in its gifts and its regards, until it encompasses the globe. How long it has taken us to realize that every endowment of talent, of influence, of wealth, is only Christ's means of helping us to 'Go ' and so to cooperate in the work of the world's redemption!

"What are the churches for but to make missionaries?

22

"What is education for but to train them?

"What is commerce for but to carry them?

"What is money for but to send them?

"What is life itself for but to fulfill the purpose of foreign missions, the purpose for which the blood-stained cross was set up on Calvary, the purpose for which God laid the floor of the firmament with its mosaic of constellations and bade the curtain of night and chaos rise at the creation! God forbid that we should glory, save in the cross of our Lord Jesus Christ!"[2]

May I add a further question:

What is prayer for but a means by which to join Christ and his purposes for redeeming his world?

4
Prayer and Its Origin

Prayer begins with God. It begins at his initiative. He not only invites, urges, and commands us to pray, he also motivates us to pray.

He initiates our seeking him in salvation. He initiates our serving him. He initiates our praying.

"You did not choose Me, but I chose you, and appointed you, that you should go and bear fruit, and that your fruit should remain, that whatever you ask of the Father in My name, He may give to you" (John 15:16, NASB).[1]

"When Thou didst say, 'Seek My face,' my heart said to Thee, 'Thy face, O Lord, I shall seek'" (Ps. 27:8, NASB).

Prayer is not our asking God for things. It is God's moving in us to pray for things he wants to do. "For it is God who is at work in you, both to will and to work for His good pleasure" (Phil. 2:13, NASB). This is the most helpful concept I hold about prayer. I do not have to badger God to do something, because he put the idea in my mind in the first place. He may have to modify my ideas or change me in the process of seeking his answer, or both. But he wants to bring me to the place of being so at one with him that I will only desire and ask for the things he wants.

"Christians," asserts missionary J. William Trimble, "are co-laborers with God—not set over against Him in an effort to get Him to do something."

Missionary Evelyn Hampton feels she is growing in understanding that prayer is largely "letting God penetrate me instead of my 'pleading' answers from God."

S. D. Gordon, author of a number of books on the Christian life, says we have been accustomed for generations to think that our asking is the thing that influences God to do. And further, that persistent, continued asking is usually necessary to persuade God to do something.

He gives an analogy about God by describing three philanthropists.

The first donor gives because he is influenced by others. If the right person or committee approaches him and skillfully presents a request, playing upon what may appeal to him, his position, his ego, what others may think, the benefits to him, etc., he may give. Though he may seem reluctant, if they persist, he finally gives more or less obligingly.

The second benefactor is the type with a benevolent heart who really wants to help others in his giving. He listens to the requests carefully and waits only long enough to be sure the cause is worthy and then decides the proper amount to give.

The third philanthropist is the rarest one. He is like the second, but he takes the initiative. He surveys the great needs everywhere, studies them in depth, decides where his money can accomplish the most good, and prepares to make bequests.

However, some might receive his money and use it unwisely or contrary to his intentions. So he establishes certain conditions to be met to guarantee that those he entrusts with the money will work for the end he wishes to see realized.

Most of us think of God as the first type of humanitarian. Yet the third one comes nearest to picturing the God who hears and answers prayer.

"Does prayer influence God?" asks Gordon. It does and it does not, he answers. It *does not* influence his *purpose*. It *does* influence his *action*. Every right thing that has been prayed for, Gordon insists, God has already purposed to do.

There are times when God awaits our consent. He has been hindered in his purposes by our lack of willingness. When we learn his purposes and make them our prayers, Gordon contends, we are giving him the opportunity to do as he has already planned.[2]

After much prayer, Earl and Veta Nell Jolley felt God's leading to Zarate, a city of 80,000 people with no Baptist church. National Christians and American friends were praying for this new work. All they had was the name of a sixty-nine-year-old Baptist who lived there.

When they contacted the man, he told them he had been praying seven years for a Baptist church in his city. One month later, a family who had been church leaders elsewhere moved to Zarate. "You can imagine the joy," exclaims Veta Nell, "ours, to have their help, and theirs, because they did not know there was a church here."

Having settled their oldest child, Mark, barely eleven, at boarding school and the MK (Missionary Kid) Home in Gwelo, Maurice and Shirley Randall were driving back to Sanyati, where Dr. Randall is a physician at the Baptist hospital. They had prayed for Mark's adjustment, as well as theirs. They did not speak or look at each other.

"The doubts and agony began to come with the tears," remembers Shirley. "Silently I prayed a desperate prayer, 'Father, if this is really right to leave a child so young, if you really want us at Sanyati hospital, if this is your will for our family at this time, speak and reassure this mother's heart.' Somewhere from the depths of my soul I whispered, 'A rainbow would help, Lord!'

"In just seconds the most magnificent rainbow spread across the road in front of our car. What peace flooded my heart as I shared with Maurice. How God loves us! Mere mortals, but his children."

Missionary Elizabeth Hale recalls hearing an earnest group of Christians during her early days in China "pleading with the Lord to do something good for someone. My heart would turn over.

"I knew the Lord was good and wanted only the best for his children. Pleading and urging God to answer is not for me," she comments. "The way that suits me is to ask that the loved one, known or unknown to me personally, may recognize and accept what God is longing to give."

The following true story has helped me understand this concept even better.

A mother phoned her daughter away at college to say that a business trip would afford her an overnight stop in the college town and a chance for a brief visit. She had made arrangements to stay with a longtime friend living near the campus.

She packed into her suitcase a beautiful evening dress she had bought for herself but had decided to give her daughter instead. The daughter had borrowed it once and hinted broadly she wished it were her own.

Delayed a couple of hours in arriving, the mother learned from her friend that the daughter had decided to go to a ball game and the aftergame activities. She had phoned to say that she would try to drop by the next morning for a brief visit before her mother left.

Hurt and disappointed, the mother decided it would not be a good time to present the dress. She felt it would be rewarding the girl for thoughtless behavior. Instead, she left the dress with her friend and told her to keep it until she notified her to give it to the daughter.

The daughter wrote apologizing for her actions and, a few weeks later, called her mother to see if she might borrow the dress for a special occasion. Could her mother mail it as soon as possible?

Explaining her earlier intentions, the mother told her she need

26

not wait several days for its arrival. The dress was at her friend's house waiting to be picked up. Further, it was a gift, not a loan. The daughter was overjoyed and the mother pleased.

This true story must be a small analogy of the way God plans to give us what we need and want, only to be thwarted by our attitudes and insensitivity.

God has many wonderful things he wants to do, but he desires to work through us. He waits for us to respond in faith and obedience.

"The eyes of the Lord run to and fro throughout the whole earth," said Hanani the seer, "to shew himself strong in the behalf of them whose heart is perfect toward him" (2 Chron. 16:9).

5
Prayer and Its Purpose

Why pray?

God *invites* us to pray. "Call to Me, and I will answer you, and I will tell you great and mighty things, which you do not know" (Jer. 33:3, NASB).

Jesus *instructs* us to pray. "Ask . . . seek . . . knock" (Matt. 7:7).

He *assumes* we will pray. "When you pray . . . " (Matt. 6:5, RSV).

His Word *encourages* us to pray. "Ye have not, because ye ask not" (Jas. 4:2).

But what is the *purpose* of praying? *Why* pray?

The basic purpose of prayer is *not* to get favors and privileges from God. "God is not a heavenly bellhop or a divine vending machine," someone has said.

"Prayer," John Killinger explains, "is not something we engage in because we wish to achieve anything.

"Prayer is communion with God. It is the act of being with him. Nothing more, nothing less.

"Now a great many things come of this—later on, when you've been at it a while.

"But in the beginning that's all it is—being with God. . . .

"You don't pray in order to achieve something. You pray in order to be with God."[1]

Though God is self-existent, all-sufficient, completely adequate in himself, and the only perfect being, I think there could be a sense in which he needs us.

Love needs an object. All of us need and want reciprocal love, including God.

Because God is person and created us for fellowship with himself, he desires us to respond to his love. Isaiah reveals, "As a groom is delighted with his bride,/So your God will delight in you" (Isa. 62:5, TEV).[2]

"Prayer," says Rosalind Rinker, "is a dialogue between two persons who love each other."[3]

The real purpose of prayer is to know God. He himself is the best answer to our prayers,[4] according to G. Campbell Morgan.

Missionary Yvonne Helton defines prayer as "a form of worship, just to enjoy talking with and getting better acquainted with God in his greatness."

Eternal life begins when we come to know God personally through a commitment to our Savior Jesus Christ. "And this is life eternal, that they may know thee, the only true God, and Jesus Christ, whom thou hast sent" (John 17:3).

This new quality of life continues and deepens as we really become acquainted with the only true God through knowing his Son.

There is a beginning knowledge. There is a deeper knowing.

Missionary Mary Saunders feels a deeper prayer life began for her "with the gift of a deepening hunger and thirst to know God."

"Let not the wise man bask in his wisdom, nor the mighty man in his might, nor the rich man in his riches," advises Jeremiah. "Let them boast in this alone: that they truly know me, and understand that I am the Lord" (Jer. 9:23-24, TLB).[5]

"Everything else is worthless," Paul proclaims, "when compared with the priceless gain of knowing Jesus Christ my Lord. I have put aside all else, counting it worth less than nothing, in order that I can have Christ" (Phil. 3:8, TLB).

Hosea expresses the desire of our hearts, "Oh, that we might know the Lord! Let us press on to know him, and he will respond to us as surely as the coming of dawn or the rain of early spring" (Hos. 6:3, TLB).

"All I want is to know Christ," we cry with Paul, "and to experience the power of his resurrection, to share in his sufferings, and become like him in his death" (Phil. 3:10, TEV).

We want to be like Mary who knew that only a few things are really necessary in this life, really only one, and she chose that most important one: to sit at Jesus' feet and get to know him (Luke 10:39-42).

Our deepest longing must be like the psalmist's: "As a deer longs for a stream of cool water, so I long for you, O God./I thirst for you, the living God" (Ps. 42:1, TEV). No surface knowledge will do. We really want to know him.

But we must seek for him as for hidden treasure (Prov. 2:4). He does not yield his most intimate thoughts and words to those who take him casually.

He promises us through Jeremiah, "You will seek me, and you will find me because you will seek me with all your heart" (Jer. 29:13, TEV).

We will never completely know him here on earth as he really is. But someday we shall see him in his completeness, face to face. Then we will know him as completely as he knows us (1 Cor. 13:12). Until then, I want to know him as intimately as I can.

"We Christians," writes James I. Packer, "are like lovers whose beloved (Christ) is away but communicates with us by letter (the Bible), while we can converse with him on the phone (prayer). One day we shall see him and communicate face to face, but for the present this is how our relationship with him must proceed."[6]

Roger Arienda, a Communist revolutionary, began to read the

Bible and accepted Christ as he was serving a twelve-year term for sedition against President Ferdinand Marcos' government in the Philippines. As he shared his faith within the prison walls, 1,600 of the 8,000 prisoners professed their belief in Christ.

Filipino and American Christians who heard how the Lord had changed him and was using him began to pray that he be pardoned. "While churches on the outside were praying for my release, I was praying, 'Lord, hold me here. I want to learn and know you more,' and I won," he said. "The Lord held me there another five years, but it was a beautiful time to learn and study."

Finally released by presidential pardon, Roger believes "it was God's time."

Shortly afterward, the former flamboyant radio commentator and political agitator had a personal conversation with President Marcos. "Mr. President, thank you for sending me to jail. Because of that I have found the Lord."[7]

It is the testimony of countless believers that *anything* that brings us to the Lord and helps us know him personally and intimately is worth it!

6
Prayer and Its Focus

There is a double meaning in saying prayer begins with God.

It begins with God in that *he* initiates it. He motivates, moves, and causes us to pray.

But also prayer begins with God in the sense that we should focus first on *him*. We must start by thinking of him rather than of ourselves, our own needs, or even of others. God is the center of the universe, not we. He runs the world. It is his, not ours.

In the example prayer Jesus teaches us to begin by thinking about God and his greatness, reverencing and cherishing the very thought of him. "Hallowed be thy name" (Matt. 6:9), is the way we commence.

I love the story of the little girl coming out of an inner-city church building one afternoon as an old gentleman was taking his daily walk. "M'dear," he asked, "what were you asking God for in there?" She looked at him in surprise. "Oh, I wasn't askin' him for anything," was her shy reply. "I was just lovin' him a little."

If we approach God for what we can get óut of him, we will be disappointed. He loves us too much to allow us to manipulate him.

If we approach prayer as a duty, a ritual, a burden, we miss the real point of prayer. "In Your presence is fullness of joy; at Your right hand there are pleasures forevermore" (Ps. 16:11, AMP).

Huber Drumwright, author of *Prayer Rediscovered,* reminds us that it was nothing short of revolutionary when Jesus spoke *to* God and *of* God as *Father.* This is hard for many of us to appreciate since we've heard God addressed as *Father* most of our lives.

The word Jesus used in the everyday Aramaic language, Dr. Drumwright points out, is the word used in the home and family, in the intimate personal living, loving relationship you and I associate with the word. "It was what a little boy would call his daddy."

"In fact," he declares, "it is so intimate and so personal that some people in our day are absolutely shocked by it when they come to realize that its equivalent in English is really 'Daddy.' People in *his* day were shocked when they heard anybody talk like that about God."

He contends the word was so precious to the early church that they kept the word in its original form, "Abba," followed by its translation, "Father" (Gal. 4:6). "Do you know that in every language in which the Bible is translated," he exclaims, "it is translated like that!"[1]

The wonder of a God, the Creator and Lord of the universe, who would allow, even invite us to call him Father! It is such a staggering thought that I cannot convert the word further to the

31

term I use for my own earthly father: "Daddy."

"All my life I have understood about the godliness of Jesus," states Peggy Hildreth, "but when I came to understand better his humanity, I found that I could talk to him in a deeper way."

We need to think of God as being at the center of our being, filling our whole heart, and possessing every part of our life. We are to fix our mind on him.

We are to love the Lord our God emotionally (with all our heart), spiritually (with all our soul), physically (with all our strength), and mentally (with all our mind) (Luke 10:27). He is to fill our being.

God who made the world and all things in it, since he is Lord of heaven and earth, does not dwell in temples made with hands (Acts 17:24). Instead he dwells in our hearts through faith (Eph 3:17), if we belong to Christ (Rom. 8:9). Therefore, the sanctuary or the holy place we meet God is in our hearts, not in the auditorium of a church building (1 Cor. 6:19).

Describing a practice she feels has strengthened her prayer life, missionary Carolyn Roberson explains how she tries to be silent before God for at least five minutes before saying a word. "I concentrate on who God is. I just stand in awe of who he is. It strengthens my life to remember constantly and daily in whose presence I stand, work, and live," she writes.

Carolyn seems to have combined the traditional and the basic meaning of the Lord's command to us through the psalmist: "Be still, and know that I am God" (Ps. 46:10).

Most of us think of being "still" as being "silent" before the Lord. And, surely, he often speaks to us when we are quiet in his presence. But the meaning behind the word seems to reflect, "stop fighting" or "cease striving." God says to us, "Give up, quit trying to do it yourself, admit you cannot and let me do it. Understand that I am in charge."

After fifteen years as a missionary, Winfield Applewhite experienced a spiritual deepening during revival among the missionaries. Instead of reading a Western to relax after a hard day of surgery as he had usually done, he began to pick up his Bible and read with a hunger he had not had before.

As months passed he noticed those who praised the Lord seemed to be the most vibrant Christians. He began seeking to learn to praise. Morning after early morning with his Bible, songbook and a cup of coffee, he would read Scriptures or hymns out loud, trying to express praise.

"One morning I was reading 'Blessed Redeemer.' Suddenly," he exulted, "it was no longer just words. I was really praising the Lord."

When the seventy disciples came back from their mission trip (Luke 10:17), they were excited over the power they experienced in using Jesus' name. Though he shared their enthusiasm and thanked God out loud in spontaneous prayer for their victories, Jesus declared it was their relationship to him that should give them joy, not their authority over evil spirits.

He told them to rejoice that their names were written in heaven.

If our motive for learning to pray is to have power, I doubt that we will ever learn. Jesus has given us authority to overcome Satan, but he warns us not to glory in mere power. He spent his entire earthly ministry trying to prove that love, not power, is the greatest force in the world.

"We need to get our perspective restored day after day. He is God and we belong to Him. Everything else is secondary to that wonderful fact. We must let it grip us, flood our hearts. We can leap down the street in its joy. The Lord is God. The Lord is *God*! And we belong to Him for ever!"[2]

7
Prayer and God's Glory

To pray for God's glory means our prayer is God-centered rather than self-centered.

A question flirts with our minds until we dare ask, "Isn't that self-centered of God to ask that we pray for answers that will glorify

33

him?" As with Eve, Satan seduces us to doubt God's motives and to picture him as arbitrary and selfish with his privileges (Gen. 3:1-5).

We are so tainted with sin that we even see God as having a form of divine egocentricity when he asks us to pray for his will and his glory.

To pray for God's glory means we pray that God's true being is revealed and recognized.

Why does he want us to pray that way?

Humility is acknowledging reality about ourselves. Paul warns, "Do not think more highly of yourself than you should" (Rom. 12:3, TEV). In other words, we are to be realistic in our appraisal of ourselves. If we can do a certain thing, it is honest humility to say we can do it.

Pride is when we exaggerate our accomplishments or our worth. Again Paul cautions, "If someone thinks he is something when he really is nothing, he is only deceiving himself" (Gal. 6:3, TEV).

God does not deceive himself. "He is all-powerful, all-knowing, all-wise, all-loving, etc.," explains Keith Parks. "Since he is perfect we cannot possibly imagine anything greater than he is or overstate his excellence. He is not asking us to think better of him than he is. He is just trying to help us see him as he actually is.

"The more we see and understand who he really is, the more we love and appreciate him. The more we truly know him, the more we become like him.

"The holiness of God simply means 'totally other.' We say 'we are *like* God' or 'Jesus became *like* us.' But the holiness of God is so totally different from human experience, we cannot even imagine what it is like. Human language is completely inadequate to describe it."

As human beings we are blinded by sin. We have tried to make God in our own image and project our human qualities on him. We need to turn it around and let him make us conform to his image and change our human qualities with his divine ones.

God cannot be self-centered or selfish. So when he asks us to pray for his glory, this is consistent with his overall plan to rescue all human beings from sin and destruction, bring us back to himself and make us like him.

Persons trying to live for God's glory will be conscious of this design even in what we consider unfortunate circumstances.

When Wycliffe Bible translator Chet Bitterman was abducted by M-19 terrorists in Colombia, Wycliffe's founder, Cameron Townsend, said, "We must begin to pray now that Chet will lead at least one of his captors to the Lord."

Chet's mother understood that "when God sends you on a mission, you cannot turn back—regardless of the circumstances." Speaking to newsmen after Chet was murdered, she declared that "the real tragedy was not the death of her son, but that a tribe of Indians would now be denied the witness of Jesus Christ."[1]

"Christ in the (Lord's) prayer teaches us that our first business in prayer is to seek with God for His victory in the world; that the deepest purpose of prayer is not that we may obtain what we need, but that God should gain that which glorifies His name."[2]

The word *glorify* has been defined as meaning "to polish" or "to remove the tarnish" until the true essence or beauty of an object can be seen.

God wants to remove the veil of sin from our eyes, or the misconception from our minds, so we can see him as he is. Then he wants to remove the tarnish of sin from our lives until we reflect the brightness and beauty of his splendor.

Each time you rub a piece of silver, it grows brighter. To me, this is the concept behind Paul's saying we are being changed into God's image from one degree of glory into another (2 Cor. 3:18).

Praying for glory to be given to God in all our circumstances, as in Romans 8:28-29, will not only help persons see God's excellence, power, fame, splendor, majesty, and honor and therefore love and worship him, but it also benefits those of us who experience the circumstances. Whatever polishes us is for our own benefit and good ultimately.

The more we see what he is like, the more like him we become. That, after all, is our ultimate purpose.

"But we Christians have no veil over our faces; we can be mirrors that brightly reflect the glory of the Lord. And as the Spirit of the

Lord works within us, we become more and more like him" (2 Cor. 3:18, TLB).

Dudley and Rebecca Phifer were appointed missionaries in 1974 to Malawi, where they served until Dudley became ill. Because malaria medication was suspected as being involved in the damage to his bone marrow, they were transferred out of the tropics to Transkei, a tribal homeland of South Africa.

Returning to Africa in September, 1979 they excitedly set about studying Xhosa language and learning the work. Dudley continued to feel well and finished a book he had started near the end of furlough: *This Light of Mine: Reflections of a First-Term Missionary.*

Then in March 1980 there began a series of virus infections, blood transfusions, and hospitalizations, followed by brief remission. In the middle of June an infection developed that caused severe chills and high fever for twenty-two days straight, during which Dudley lost twenty-five pounds, and resulted in another hospitalization with transfusions and intravenous antibiotics.

"He sort of 'limped along' through July," wrote Rebecca, "losing more weight and feeling generally weak. But through it all he clung to the hope that the Lord might give him some more time to serve in Transkei. He continued to preach at Norwood any time he was able to crawl out of bed at all.

"This last month has been really hard, but the Lord has been teaching us he did not call us to make life easy. He called us to glorify him in whatever circumstances we find ourselves and our prayer these days is, 'Lord, let us bring honor and glory to your name whatever happens to us.'"

In August, Dudley was hospitalized in Cape Town with acute myelocytic leukemia. Tests showed the bone marrow had deteriorated dramatically. Doctors were not sure that he would ever leave Cape Town, but treatment improved his condition sufficiently for him to make the two-day trip to Houston.

Admitted to M.D. Anderson hospital, Dudley went home to be with the Lord eleven days later. Rebecca expressed her feelings in a letter to friends and family.

"First, I want to thank the Foreign Mission Board for allowing us to go back to Africa. A few people thought we were foolish to go back under the circumstances, and we know that the board did not easily make the decision to let us return.

"But I thank them for understanding about our deep sense of call and for being supportive in so many ways. Though we were only in Transkei eleven months, I feel that we made a contribution. Dudley's sheer determination to serve as long as he lived was an inspiration to many.

"The doctor at M.D. Anderson hospital also supported our desire to return to the mission field. He realized that what was going to happen was indeed going to happen regardless of where we were and knew it was terribly important to us to return to Africa.

"The last two years have been difficult for us in many ways. I have spent a lot of time grieving because it seemed that I was not going to have the opportunity of growing old with Dudley. But after pleading with the Lord to spare him, a few months ago we realized the Lord had brought us both to the point of saying, 'Lord, we don't know why this is happening. We wouldn't choose it to happen, but it does seem to be happening to us. Therefore, let us glorify you in it.'

"Finally, I just want to praise the Lord for the twenty beautiful years he gave me with Dudley. This gentle, loving, humble man made a tremendous impact on my life. At his funeral I breathed a prayer saying, 'Thank you, Lord, that our children had the kind of father about whom such wonderful things can be said.' Better to have had Dudley Phifer for twenty years than anyone else for a hundred!"

"They had a tremendous testimony among the Africans," declares Davis L. Saunders, the Phifers' area director. "The leaders have said to me, 'Send us more missionaries just like the Phifers.'"

Leaving a daughter in college, Rebecca and her other three children have returned to Malawi.

Writing after getting settled again in her adopted country, Rebecca describes her praying:

"Prayer these days is more a commitment of things to God. It is no longer so much asking God to change circumstances for me or for others. It is rather saying to him, 'Lord, what do you have to teach me in these circumstances? How can I bring glory to you through them, even if they are not ones I would choose for myself?'

"I am learning to rest in him and say, 'OK, Lord, here is the way things are. You already know all about it and how it is going to turn out. Work through all of this to bring glory ultimately to yourself.'

"If I am praying for myself or for someone else, I ask God to make me or the other person more conformed to the image of his dear Son through the experience."

8
Prayer and Awakening

A cold chill ran down my spine. I reread the words. God said to Jeremiah, "As for you, do not pray for this people, or lift up cry or prayer for them, and do not intercede with me; for I do not hear you" (Jer. 7:16, RSV).

At various times and in varying degrees I have been concerned for our country and our sinfulness, for Christians and our cold, worldly ways. I have prayed for national revival, but not consistently and not often, as of necessity, with the burden that it *must* come.

The Old Testament repeats the cycle again and again. God blessed his people. Instead of being grateful, they were ungrateful, sinful, and rebellious. God warned, judged, and punished. His people then repented and returned to God.

As a child hearing these Bible stories, I wondered why the children of Israel did not wake up, learn their lesson, stay close to God, enjoy his blessings, and escape punishment.

As an adult living through the same cycle several times in the life of our nation, I now understand how it could happen better than I did as a child.

A prophet stood before his people, confronting them with their needs and God's message. Jeremiah was the "weeping prophet," but he was also a praying one. Because of his compassion, he interceded for his people's sins.

The root of all evils among the Israelites was their worship of idols. They had replaced the living God with gods of materialism, lust, and illicit sex. They used his name without meaning. They went through the motions of worship while their hearts were far from him. They misused his day. They ignored his commands, precepts, and ways. They thought he didn't know or care how they lived. They believed he was too patient to punish them. They felt they could offer leftovers for sacrifices and placate his displeasure with tips. They ignored his warnings, thinking the prophets were fanatics or unpatriotic, mentally ill or mistaken.

God had called and pleaded, warned and threatened, shaken and punished his people. Still they paid no attention. They were so far gone in disobedience and corruption that God no longer expected repentance and returning. He had made up his mind. Judgment must fall. Jeremiah was told that praying would do no good.

In 1970 a young man told me, "Mrs. Parks, in ten years all the rules your generation has made will be gone . . . gone!" "Unhappily, Jack," I replied, "you may be right. But do not forget one thing. The God who made those rules will not be gone. You do not break his rules. You break yourself on his rules."

In the years since, I have watched both predictions coming true—his and mine. Few nations with a Judeo-Christian heritage have degenerated so quickly as the U.S. As Christians we have sat back and watched with utter dismay as standards of morality and decency have been trampled. As a friend, I have witnessed the slow destruction of the young man.

One can read daily newspapers, watch television, attend movies, look at magazines, listen to talk about townspeople, and learn graphically more about the corruption and degradation of our nation than I could describe. If God lets our nation go unpunished for our unbridled wickedness, he will not be true to his Word. If our nation does not decline because of our sin, we will be the first nation in history to break the precedent.

If we do not pray and God's Holy Spirit does not bring conviction of sin, sincere repentance, and deep revival, he may toss us on the junk heap of nations and move on to find people he can use more readily in accomplishing his purposes. Have we passed the point of no return or can God still bring us back? We will not know until we pray constantly and fervently for awakening or until judgment falls.

Walker F. Knight writes that "revivals alter lives of individuals; awakenings alter the world view of a whole people or culture.[1]

"John Havlik believes four vital characteristics herald an era of awakening: it is a time of social stress or change; God's people have become complacent and cold; many people have become dissatisfied with conditions as they are in society; and thousands of people are praying for an awakening."[2]

Dr. A. T. Pierson said, "There has never been a spiritual awakening in any country or locality that did not begin in united prayer."[3]

"We must not forget what was said by Jonathan Edwards," recalls J. Edwin Orr. 'Promote explicit agreement and visible union of God's people in extraordinary prayer.'

"What do we mean by extraordinary prayer?" Orr asks. "We share in ordinary prayer in regular worship services, before meals, and the like. But when people are found getting up at six in the morning to pray, or having a half night of prayer until midnight, or giving up their lunchtime to pray at a noonday prayer meeting, that is extraordinary prayer.

"But it must be united and concerted. A Baptist . . . an Anglican . . . or a Presbyterian [must] recognize each other as fraternal intercessors."[4]

But we must get beyond the motive of saving our nation and our own necks. There must be the motive of desiring God's glory in our lives and his salvation for our lost friends. In a glorious song service at church one night, as I adored the Lord and enjoyed joining in his praises, I longed for my lost friends to have this kind of joyous experience with him. This must become our reason for revival, rather than just escaping judgment.

All along the problem and the remedy for our nation have been

40

with "us," not "them." We have blamed secular humanism, amoral education and government, godless media, the "leftists," the "rightists," the "liberals," . . . everybody, and anybody else but *us, Christians*. At first, we felt if *they* would straighten up, *we* would be fine.

Then we tried to coexist. If *they* would just leave us alone, we could remain aloof, withdraw to our own churches and schools, raise our children so they would not be contaminated, and we would leave them alone. As they have encroached more and more and will not leave us alone, many of us have abandoned our passivity and are trying political means to make them conform to our standards.

When will we learn that such means do not work? When will we admit *our* wickedness is the problem, not just *theirs*? When will we realize *we* have had the solution all the time?

The recipe given to Solomon in Old Testament times is just as valid today as then. "If I shut up the heavens so that there is no rain, or if I command the locust to devour the land, or if I send pestilence among my people. [In other words, inflation, poor economic conditions, and epidemics of illness like cancer? Heart disease?] If *my people* [not those who do not profess to believe in me], which are *called by my name*, shall humble *themselves*, and pray, and seek my face, and turn from *their* wicked ways; then will I hear from heaven, and will forgive *their* sin, and will heal *their* land" (2 Chron. 7:13-14, author's italics).

"If only people would so plead for the church! For God is not in our midst. We worship the golden calves of material prosperity, of worldly prestige and respectability, of academic degrees and political power. Our successes are less the product of the Holy Spirit than of our technical proficiency.

"The world can easily understand how well we do. We have the machinery and we know how to use it. No supernatural explanation of our expansion is needed. Who needs God? He is our figurehead, our logo. His photograph has the place of honor in our corporation board rooms. But he is chairman emeritus; and, we, unlike Israel, do not even miss him.[5]

As modern-day American Christians, we have one of the main

idols the Israelites had. So did the Ephesians, to whom Paul wrote, "Since you are God's people, it is not right that any matters of sexual immorality or indecency or greed should even be mentioned among you. . . . You may be sure that no one who is immoral, indecent, or greedy (for greed is a form of idolatry) will ever receive a share in the Kingdom of Christ and of God" (Eph. 5:3,5, TEV).

We do not admit to being covetous or greedy, but who among us today can say we are not tainted with materialism. It is the doctrine that says comfort, pleasure, and wealth are the highest goals in life. No one more so than Christians in our society today believes that. We may not be guilty of sexual immorality, but we are not innocent of being materialistic. It is an idol. It is our Baal. We are guilty. We have sinned.

We can admit it, seek God's face as of necessity, turn from our idols and wicked ways, and God promises he will hear, forgive us, and heal our land.

We have the key to our country's well-being.

We also have the key for the gospel's proclamation to the world.

If we do not pray for ourselves and our nation now, we won't need to pray for missions in the future.

We will become like countries who once had the gospel but did not live it. They turned inward and did not share it. They lived for themselves, spent their means selfishly, and came under the judgment of God.

9
Prayer and World Politics

"The man who mobilizes the Christian church to pray will make the greatest contribution to the world's evangelization in history," Andrew Murray is quoted as saying.

Many Christians have never taken prayer seriously, much less really thought of sharing Jesus Christ with every single person in the world.

Compare the vision and zeal of most Christians with that of political revolutionaries. Having realized they were jeopardizing Chinese Christians whose new government suspected that they were American spies, the missionaries applied and were waiting for government permission to leave China. The Christian university where Lorene Tilford taught had been closed. Nightly she and other missionaries watched the organized parades as thousands of young people marched carrying torches and banners. "Down with Imperialism." "Stamp out Colonialism." "Go home, Americans."

"Bye, Miss Tilford," shouted a friendly marcher. Squinting in the dim light and scanning the mob, she recognized a former student. "Bye," he waved, smiling, "we'll see you when we get to America."

She was amused. *He really believes he will,* she thought. Then she sobered. Who could predict? After all, no one had taken them seriously when their movement began in the hills of interior China. A small corps of revolutionaries joined by malcontents and dissidents had started their sweep across China, their numbers swelling with idealistic youth as they went. They had marched barefooted and shabby, in rain and the cold, chanting as they went, "We're hungry! We're cold! But we're changing the world!" And they had taken over China, the world's most populous country!

Who could know or predict where it would stop? Maybe someday he *would* see her in her homeland!

Arriving in America before reassignment, she called Christians and churches to account. "The Communists have their manifesto. They believe they can win the world and they have set out to do it! We Christians have had our Commission (Matt. 28:18-20) for two millenia. What are we doing to obey it?"

Some in our churches are not even aware of our commission. Many more have forgotten, ignored, or thought it impossible, or at least impractical. Even those of us taking it seriously wonder if it's really possible to tell *every* person in the *whole* world.

But if the Communists can win as much of the world with force and human strength as they have, what could Christians do in the love and power of the Almighty God? If we yearned for lost persons sincerely? If we loved the Lord supremely? If we believed his commands and promises implicitly?

World conquest begins with prayer. Without it, plans and strategy are useless. "Not by might, nor by power, but by my spirit, saith the Lord of hosts" (Zech. 4:6).

Pitted against a lost world like David against Goliath, the giant, we must say, "You come to me with a sword, a spear, and a javelin, but I come to you in the name of the Lord of hosts, the God of the armies of Israel, . . . the Lord will deliver you up into my hands . . . that all the earth may know that there is a God in Israel, and that all . . . may know that the Lord does not deliver by sword or by spear; for the battle is the Lord's and He will give you into our hands" (1 Sam. 17:45-47, NASB).

How can we accomplish such an impossible assignment? We can't. But the one who made the assignment to go and make disciples of all nations is also the one who told us, "All power is given to me in heaven and in earth" (Matt. 28:18).

Daniel exulted in God's greatness. "Blessed be the name of God forever and ever, for he alone has all wisdom and all power. World events are under his control. He removes kings and sets others on their thrones. The God of heaven will set up a kingdom that will never be destroyed; no one will ever conquer it. It will shatter all these kingdoms into nothingness, but it shall stand forever, indestructible" (Dan. 2:20-21a, 44, TLB).

How can we win the world to our Lord? We can't. We are powerless. But Job, in recounting how God created the heavens and the earth, divided light from darkness, set boundaries for the ocean, and controls the sea, exclaims about him: "These are some of the minor things he does, merely a whisper of his power" (Job 26:14, TLB). If those are his whispers, he asks, who could withstand his thunder?

A small book, *Shaping History Through Prayer and Fasting* by Derek Prince, sets forth the way Christians can be used in God's saving purposes. He focuses primarily on the disciplines of prayer and fasting.

Paul tells us to pray for all men everywhere, for kings and those in authority so that we may live quiet and peaceful lives in all godliness and honesty. Such praying pleases God, he explains, for he longs for all men to have the opportunity to be saved (1 Tim. 2:1-4). Our praying is linked to the salvation of all persons.

We are to pray for heads of state and government officials to speed the gospel on its way. We can pray for changes in laws and official policies that impede the spread of God's kingdom.

One of the most exciting answers to long-term praying occurred in Spain in July 1980, when constitutional guarantees for religious freedom were given. For years many Christians around the world had prayed for an end to religious persecution.

"Many of us," admits missionary Betty Law, "had not even dared pray for constitutional guarantees. We were just praying for religious toleration and were thankful for the increasing freedom from persecution." She believes the timing of God's answer has been perfect, arriving just as second, third, and fourth generation evangelicals are trained for leadership and able to assume more financial responsibility for the work.

What can a small mission church do when its members recognize that unless God works a miracle their work in a new and promising area will grind to a halt? Can their prayers change state law?

In two years, according to missionary Maxie Kirk, the mission effort in a Rio residential area had grown from a single Bible study group to several such groups and children's Bible clubs gathering both in homes of the poor and in exclusive high-rise condominiums of the wealthy. They began meeting together for worship services in a rented building. The fellowship of believers from diverse socioeconomic backgrounds could be a testimony of God's accepting grace.

They sought approval to build a church building on a centrally located lot donated by Brazilian Baptists. Plans for a simple structure passed the strict building code, but the zoning board refused permission. Officials had interpreted a law which did not grant explicit permission for churches in a residential area as prohibiting them.

To change the law, the church began a prayer vigil that was to last two years. Other Christians who shared the vision for new and needed church sites joined the praying.

In a special prayer meeting two years after the first one, church leaders and pastor defined again their needs before the Lord. Within the week, word came from a Christian layman working with state legislators that the zoning law had been amended to allow churches, schools, and service facilities to build in residential areas.

The small, but growing mission church was the first to be approved by the zoning commissioner.

It was announced that the largest Baptist church in the capital city of a Central American nation was to be razed by the government as the location for a monument that could be seen from sea, land, and air. Also condemned for clearing was the lot containing a pastor's residence.

At stake were both money and public perception of evangelicals. The government was offering compensation of $8,000 for property which had appreciated to a value of over one million dollars. No recompense was to be made for the buildings. No appeals could be made. Christians were asked to pray.

The decision was reported still firm the day before the final hearing. Groups continued to pray.

A scheduled second hearing was not held. The government issued a terse statement: "Decision reversed."

The writer of Proverbs explains, "The Lord controls the mind of a king as easily as he directs the course of a stream" (Prov. 21:1, TEV).

10
Prayer and Uprooting

God does not ask his followers to *prepare* nations or men for the gospel. He does that. He uses war, natural calamity, social upheaval, political revolution, and trauma of every description. I am not sure which of these God sends or allows. But I do know he uses them. We have seen how crises in the lives of persons we know have brought non-Christians to trust Christ as Savior or backslidden Christians back to the Lord or to a new spiritual commitment.

Daniel T. Niles of Sri Lanka (Ceylon), speaking in 1966 to a group assembled at the International English service in Jakarta, Indonesia, explained the concept. It became "truth that mattered" because my adopted country was in a power struggle be...een Communist and Army forces to secure the government. The outcome would determine our destiny.

God does the plowing. We do the sowing.

When people are uprooted from their traditional sources of security, from all they have lived for and clung to, then they grasp for something secure. They will hear new ideas. This, said Niles, is when we as Christians must be faithful and diligent to sow the gospel seed in freshly-plowed ground.

God plows the hearts of men and nations. We must be quick to plant the seed.

Persons who move are more open to overtures for friendship, invitations to church, and new ventures during the first six months in a new place than later when they get settled, find friends, and set up their routine. As soon as we see the moving van in our neighborhood, we must hurry to plant the seeds of prayer, love, concern, and witness.

As quickly as we get news of war or fighting, earthquake or flood, drought or starvation, national elections or a government overthrown, we must be quick to intercede for the nation or persons affected. We may be impressed to pray for peace, but perhaps persons will turn to God only through the confusion, pain, or misery caused by the "uprooting." It is of primary importance that God accomplish his purposes and spiritual peace come as hearts are opened to him and his Son.

In the fifties I was a young and immature missionary on furlough from a responsive country. I heard missionaries from a "hard" country tell of difficult conditions coupled with very little response. The country seemed hopeless to me. Winston Crawley, Southern

Baptist missions leader, in explaining why different missionaries feel called to different countries, declared that some feel challenged by the "hardness" of a certain field. "And, in that case," he said, "they would be 'tickled to death' in _____ [the aforementioned country]."

Difficult living conditions might not be so bad if persons were being saved and results of my ministry were visible. But to endure *both* physical and spiritual hardness would not have been my choice.

I prayed a few feeble "mustard seed" prayers for that country but still wondered how in the world God could do anything with people so hardened to the gospel.

Since my faithless thoughts a quarter of a century ago, there have been famines, tidal waves, grinding poverty, and, finally, war in that nation. Also missionaries have been faithfully sowing the seed year in and year out. Some stayed voluntarily during the war and suffered with their people.

In recent times on furloughs and in newsletters those missionaries tell of tens, dozens, and even whole villages of persons reading the Bible, responding to God's love, and saying, "I believe in Jesus."

Last year that nation's Baptist Union reported a 39 percent increase in its churches.

Now I pray with more faith and vision for the "hard" countries.

Millie Lovegren, whose missionary father was imprisoned when the Communist government came to power in China, had grown up there as an MK and gone back as a missionary herself. She mourned for her adopted people when she had to leave. "China was so responsive to the gospel," she said. "I could not understand why God would allow China to close to missionaries."

Some years later a Chinese friend living in Hong Kong was able to visit her mainland China birthplace. She returned telling how the temples and churches had been turned into granaries, offices, and apartment buildings. She had not seen one idol or joss stick. "Gradually I realized," declared Millie, "that what years of Christian missions had never been able to do, the Communist government had done in a few brief years. With the idols gone, I began to have hope and to pray that the spiritual vacuum created would open the way for Jesus Christ."

Retired China missionary Olive Lawton quotes another missionary after his recent visit there: "In 1949 there were an estimated one million Protestant Christians in China. Today the Christian population is estimated to be between four and six million. We wrongly thought the door was shut to the gospel in China for thirty years. But God never left China. God, the Holy Spirit, was testing and purifying his church. The amazing number of new believers is evidence of his power."

The nineteen-year-old Cambodian girl had escaped into Thailand with 100 others after an unbelievable journey through miles of jungle, canals, mountains, rivers, and a stretch of ground covered with thorns. Most were either barefoot or wore flimsy sandals.

They had threaded their way through Communist soldiers and harsh forces of nature. Crossing a valley between two high mountain ranges, the struggling little band could see nothing in a midnight-like darkness. "We did not know where to step," the girl told missionary Maxine Stewart. Suddenly hundreds of swarming fireflies gave light enough to see the path and reach the next mountain.

Disorientation and exhaustion delayed and threatened their escape to freedom. Hallucinating, the girl once thought she was seeing the ocean. Many of the group collapsed on reaching Thailand. The girl had to be carried to the refugee camp and required two months' medical treatment to recover.

When she was transferred to the camp where missionaries worked, she agreed to attend a Christian meeting. As she entered the bamboo chapel she exclaimed and pointed to a picture on the wall.

"'I know that old man. He is the one who led us and showed the way to Thailand and freedom.'

"She was pointing to a picture of Jesus."[1]

Who can know or understand what God is doing or preparing to do in troubled countries like Cambodia?

Who can know what he could or would do if we prayed for Christians in those lands, for their governments, and for his purposes to be wrought?

With the psalmist we cry, O God, "Surely the wrath of man shall praise You" (Ps. 76:10, AMP).

11
Prayer and Closed Doors

Praying does not relieve Christians from going to take the gospel. Instead, prayer will produce laborers—ourselves and others. Prayer will multiply and anoint the labor of those who go. Prayer can overcome obstacles, real or imagined. It can find ways over barriers and through closed doors.

What of unseen barriers? Where missionaries work, but with few results? Could it be the walls have not come down because Christians have not prayed for them to fall?

"Please share with us two heavy burdens," pleaded Ronald and Evelyn Hill. "One is the continuing slow response of the Thai people. Though they are listening, asking questions, and seem hungrier than ever before, still so few are making commitments to Christ. Some say the reason is that they have such an abundant and easy life in this fertile country. Others say our Thai Christian vocabulary does not communicate accurately. Still others say it is the foreignness of Christianity: it comes in too Western a garb.

"But we can't see any reason for the lack of response but spiritual.

"Our second burden is that so many Christians 'fall away.' Though we're baptizing some, each year about an equal number fall away, so that the membership stays almost the same.

"We need your focused prayer in two specific ways. The first is for a spiritual breakthrough. We have never had one like has happened in several other countries. Will you help us pray?

"Our prayer is like David's: 'Part your heavens, O Lord, and come down' (Ps. 144:5, NIV). He did. In Jesus Christ. He has. Many times in history. He will. If we truly call on him.

"Second is a prayer for laborers. We need ten more missionary couples for church planting while we can still get them in. We need young Thai pastors to replace an older generation and lay leaders to lead in some seventy-five small groups we hope will become churches.

"Our hearts' desire is that the Thai may come in large numbers to know our Savior. Yet even with heavy hearts we experience deep joy in the privilege of being here in this strategic place and in having so many of you there stand with us in the front lines of prayer."

What of places missionaries *cannot* go?

The Holy Spirit does not need a visa to enter any country. He is already there. He knows no Iron or Bamboo Curtains. Islam, Buddhism, Hinduism, traditional Christianity, atheism, animism are no obstacles to him. Missionaries do not "take Christ" to a country. He is already there. They go to interpret him.

Could it be that we have been unaware that God's plan for reaching those we consider inaccessible involves Christians interceding for them?

On their last furlough, Les and Jan Hill, missionaries in the Philippines, were confronted with the challenge of the "hidden" peoples of the world (those who are untouched by contact with missionaries or even Christian neighbors).

"It seemed the only logical thing to do was pray that they too might be saved," Jan explained. "God laid on my heart India, China, and the Muslim nations. I prayed specifically that God would raise up pastors and evangelists.

"Since then I have heard of a recent breakthrough among Hindus and Muslims in certain places. Hearing also of the growth of the underground church in China from time to time has encouraged me to keep praying.

"No one is more conscious than missionaries," she continues, "of the time difference here and on the other side of the earth. When I go to bed Sunday nights, I pray for my children and loved ones back home just getting ready to go to church.

"Several years ago while thinking about this I realized that in every time zone people were gathering to worship somewhere, hour after hour. It must be a delight to the Lord to hear praise directed to him through song and sermon throughout the day (Ps. 113:1-3).

"Here in the Philippines we live near the beginning of each new day. God has taught me to take my post early every Sunday morning as a 'watchman on the wall' (see Isa. 62:6-7), praying that through the day, throughout the time zones throughout the world, the word of God will be proclaimed in great power. I pray for pastors and missionaries to go and preach in spirit and truth. I pray that the word will reach those who have never heard and that a great harvest of souls will be brought to the Lord.

"I am sure there are those who pray for the lost of the world, but my prayer is that there will be many more who will take their post on the Lord's day, in their own time zones and pray for the 'hidden' peoples."

Because Islam has traditionally been militant, resistant, and antagonistic to the gospel, many have considered it an impenetrable barrier. An interview with an independent missionary, whose identity and location cannot be revealed because of likely repercussions and persecution, gives witness to a significant moving of the Holy Spirit among Muslims.

"We see the Holy Spirit moving with power, jumping the wall of Islam," he declares. "We are seeing that many of the Muslims coming to Christ do not do so as a result of studying Scripture, being convicted, and saved in our traditional Christian terms. Rather it seems as though the Holy Spirit seeks them out, points a finger at them and calls them out of Islam into a life of great sacrifice. Many risk and some give their very lives.

"Many come to Christ because of a supernatural experience. They hear a voice, dream a dream, have a vision. There is a combination of circumstances that is so compelling in their lives that it totally changes their life orientation.

"When Muslims talk about seeing the Lord Jesus in a vision, they all describe the same person. They have no background of Christian art to guide the picture symbol they might have of Jesus, but they all describe him in the same terms."

The missionary tells of one young man, an excellent student who loved to debate. He began debating the local Muslim priest who continually attacked Christians. In order to take the opposite view he became acquainted with some Christians to get more information about their beliefs. In doing so, he said, "I grew to love the Lord Jesus." He was baptized without his parents' knowledge. That night he had a vision.

"The Lord Jesus stood beside me," he related. "He beckoned me to rise. He smiled at me and said, '_____, today you have been baptized with water, but I am going to baptize you with the Holy Spirit. But before I baptize you with the Holy Spirit, something always has to die.' I looked around and, to my amazement, saw the body of a man lying on the ground beside me. I looked more carefully. I recognized the features—they were my own.

"I looked back to the Lord. He smiled at me and held out his arms. He embraced me closer, closer, closer, and then to my amazement I recognized we were no longer separate. He was in me, I was in him, and then I knew what you Christians mean when you say 'Christ in me, the hope of glory.'"

PRAYER ON THE LORD'S DAY

On this your day, O Lord, I pray that your Word will go out to the ends of the earth, for now is the day of salvation.

May it be proclaimed through music and song that stirs the souls of men and women and draws them to you.

May continual praise be lifted up to you in every time zone throughout the day.

May your message of love and reconciliation through Christ be preached in power and strength in every language of every nation.

May each of your children be busy about their Father's business with a faith that does not falter.

May the good news be as newsworthy as the front page of today's paper.
May it be the topic of discussion among the rich and the poor, the powerful and the meek.

May it shatter every barrier and capture every heart. And may people everywhere bow and confess on bended knee that Jesus is Lord. Jesus is Lord. Amen.[1]

—JAN HILL

12
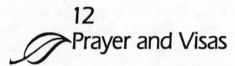Prayer and Visas

Few things are more vital to mission work overseas than visas. Without this official document from the host government, a missionary cannot enter the country to which God has called him.

An American has no trouble getting a United States passport to leave this country and, in most cases, a visa for each country he wishes to visit or pass through. But receiving a visa to enter, live, and work in a foreign country is a different matter.

Since they have reciprocal agreements, many governments are careful not to alienate each other by refusing entrance to the other's citizens.

Some governments are officially anti-Western or anti-Christian. Missionaries are not allowed. Some, strongly influenced by the nation's major religion which may be non-Christian or non-Protestant, seek to discourage evangelical Christians entering to propagate their faith.

Some nations see missionaries as a holdover of colonialism. Developing nations may feel that having missionaries working in their country implies inferiority, an admission of needing help. Several see missionaries as competing for local employment and financial resources, when, in fact, their salaries and work funds bring dollars into the country.

Delays or refusal in granting visas may be caused by official government policy or by individual officials who are unsympathe-

54

tic. The reason could be bureaucratic inefficiency or indifference. Many governments lack the computer and technical facilities to handle the process quickly.

An unfriendly official may employ delaying tactics such as extended procedures and extreme red tape. There might be a tacit expectation of money to speed the system. Whereas we would consider this a bribe and unacceptable, the person from another culture might understand it as normal and acceptable.

In some cases, ecumenical Christian groups are consulted by government agencies. If they view a new group with suspicion or as competition, their opposition may bar or delay entrance.

Whatever the government's attitude, missionaries and short-term volunteers must accept that they are guests of that country and that a visa is a privilege granted, not a right.

"The task of a missionary," declared Catholic bishop James Edward Walsh, who spent twelve years in a Chinese Communist prison, "is to go to a place where he is not wanted but needed, and to remain until he is not needed but wanted."

Many of us have prayed for missionaries seeking entrance to places they were not wanted. Quite a number of missionaries are serving where God called them because we helped "pray them in."

For two and a half years prayer was asked for Norman and Jeanie Wood as they tried to enter a country. Continuing to feel led there, though visas were repeatedly denied, they finally set a "cutoff" date when they would have to take another assignment. The day before they were to be reassigned, temporary permission to enter was granted.

A year later visa renewal looked bleak as hostile officials were threatening expulsion. Again, Christians prayed and the decision was reversed. Those of us who prayed felt we had a part in getting them in and then in keeping them there. As this book goes to press, the process is being repeated.

Jeanie explained, "With each work permit, we faced the same problem. We had to wait . . . wait . . . wait, and, just when we needed it, God supplied the permit. God is teaching us patience and the virtue of waiting on him."

Bill and Elba Womack first entered the country where they serve in 1972 just as the nation's governing body was ending debate on missionaries and faith healers. Though they had complied with regulations, they were told they could not stay. Arriving Friday night, they asked permission to stay and fly out Monday.

"There were people all over Missouri, Texas, Mississippi, and Alabama praying we'd get work permission," Womack said. They were able to stay nine months before they received a six-month permit. "People kept praying. Our next permit was for a year. They kept praying and we received a year and a half. They kept praying and we received three years. Then two, then two. It has been ten years. People's prayers are the answer!"

Charles and Mary Love had told the Lord they needed to know a certain number of weeks before leaving on furlough whether they would be returning. Since they were the only missionaries of their board in that country, they needed to sell properties held by the mission if they were not returning. Officials would give no answer.

"We spent a year's furlough not knowing if we could return," recalls Mary. All year they asked churches to pray for God's will regarding their plans. When furlough was over, Charles flew back to see if they could reenter. Permission was granted. A letter was carried in their state paper thanking those who enabled them to return by praying.

"We learned you cannot give God deadlines," Mary says. "He opens doors when he is ready. We learned to rest in the Lord and trust him."

Two weeks before Otis and Martha Brady were to transfer to a country they thought was "very open," a letter came announcing the government's decision that no new missions could begin work.

"We had not anticipated this," Martha points out, "but we began to ask those we knew who really would, to pray about this."

Two days before they got the letter God had confirmed the Scripture to them, "I will go before thee, and make the crooked places straight" (Isa. 45:2). "It was like he said, 'Hang on to this,'" she remembers.

The Bradys proceeded to their country and began an eight-month effort to get permission for starting work. "The waiting was not passive. It was as much a part of what God was doing as anything else," they explained. "We know that was because of people's prayers.

"We can look back and see how God allowed this time to establish vital relationships with other Christian groups. Had we had permission to start churches immediately we would not have done this.

"We could see God's hand in the delay," declares Brady. It gave them time to understand that existing groups were working mainly with middle- and upper middle-class people. They determined needs and began chapels in lower socioeconomic areas when permission was given.

"In a new mission field missionaries are handicapped because most people in our churches don't know anything about the country and do not know how to pray. But the Lord gave us some real prayer supporters. We think that is why the country has become so responsive."

In one major mission field, missionaries have worked under the stress of continuing rumors and threats of eviction. Visa extension requests remain under consideration for months or are stamped "Temporary" or "Six months only." It is difficult to make long-range plans either personally or for their work. The uncertainty adds to the pressures they face and can be a factor in the lack of effectiveness or even in resignations.

One benefit of this instability is to give urgency to training and discipling national Christians quickly and preparing churches to stand alone.

Missionary Ed Sanders assesses their situation: "If we allowed our circumstances to determine our spiritual and emotional health, things would look pretty bleak. But this should not be the case.

Our Lord would remind us that we are just sojourners here in the first place.

"He is in control of this and every situation. He sleeps not, neither does he rest. This is our assurance! The future has been clearly revealed. The details of our involvement are not as clearly revealed, but that is part of the joy and excitement of living by faith. God writes the chapter heading, then fills in the story line by line and word by word through our everyday experience in his grace."

13
Prayer as Intercession

With God we can change the world. We are partners in his design. He chooses us and blesses us so that through us he can bless others. This is the whole profound, yet simple missionary concept throughout the Bible beginning at Genesis 12:3. He loves us but does not want his love to stop there. He wants to love through us so that every other person in the world can know his love and be blessed.

We can bring good news to the poor, proclaim liberty to the captives and recovery of sight to the blind. We can liberate the oppressed and announce that the Lord has come to save his people (Luke 4:18-19).

The same ministry Jesus had on earth becomes ours when we identify with him in his death for our sins and his resurrection for our new life. It is the same ministry he still carries on through his Spirit on earth, as he is seated at the right hand of God, constantly interceding for us (Heb. 7:25).

Through us God can change men's hearts. Through us God can transform circumstances. Through us God can revolutionize nations. When we pray, it is as if we were opening a window so that God's love may flow to other people.

A current religious teaching is that we need to learn to pray on earth as grooming for reigning with God in heaven. My personal conviction is that we need to learn to pray because we are already reigning with him in spiritual matters here on earth.

We have been made a "kingdom of priests to serve our God" (Rev. 5:10, TEV). We have been chosen to stand before men for God and to "proclaim the wonderful acts of God" (1 Pet. 2:9, TEV). In Ephesians Paul says that the God of our Lord Jesus Christ "raised Christ from death and seated him at his right hand in the heavenly world" (1:20, TEV) and that those of us who have been saved by his grace are in union with Christ and have been raised up to rule with him in the heavenly world (2:5-6, TEV).

We are not just being groomed for later. We are at work now. We can make a difference in the world today. We are getting on-the-job training for bringing Christ's kingdom to reality now, not later in heaven but as it is now in heaven.

Paul tells us how to do it. "You have been raised to life with Christ, so set your hearts on the things that are in heaven, where Christ sits on his throne at the right side of God. Keep your minds fixed on things there, not on things here on earth" (Col. 3:1-2, TEV).

We can change our world now by keeping our minds on Christ's kingdom. It must be our priority. We must live and work for it at all times.

There is no higher form of petition than intercession. It is self-forgetfulness and love concentrated. It is the attitude Paul recommended, "look out for one another's interests, not just for your own" (Phil. 2:4, TEV).

My favorite definition of intercession comes from Hallesby: "To pray is to tell Jesus what we lack. Intercession is to tell Jesus what we see that others lack."[1] Beautiful!

We do not tell him how to meet the need. We just tell him what it is.

Intercession expresses love for others.
Mrs. O. C. Ellis suggests we let a person know when we intercede for him, just as Jesus told Peter he was praying for him.

59

Missionary Karen Quimby would verify this practice. "A best friend in Christ prays for me personally every day. This gives me unbelievable strength and humbles me at the same time."

Karen tells of another friend who taught her a lot about prayer by a very simple act. Though she herself was a very busy mother and teacher, the friend sent a card saying, "For your birthday I give you one hour weekly for prayer," and offering to keep her three toddlers so she could spend the time alone with God.

"She knew I had very little time for myself or the Lord. That was the beginning of spiritual growth and maturing for me and the astounding realization that God answers prayer." It was also when God began preparing her heart for missionary service.

Intercessory prayer brings victories.

Having worked with South Carolina Woman's Missionary Union seven years, missionary Janie House had heard many stories of prayer answers on missionaries' birthdays. Though she had a good day, nothing spectacular happened on hers.

In the two weeks following her birthday, however, she began to be aware of some changes in herself. "It seems priorities are getting sorted and some needs for self-control are suddenly being met. I believe it is in answer to people's prayers for me and I am really excited. These small, personal changes are really miraculous— things I have not been able to do in my own power."

Intercessors can share missionaries' problems.

A friend in America prayed two years for missionary Roberta Fisher as she worked her way through culture shock. Identifying with her problems of nagging illness, wearing climate, and discouraging living conditions as best she could, the friend shared Scriptures and wrote out the prayers she was praying on her behalf. They all seemed related to what Bobbi was experiencing at the time.

"I would feel like giving in to pressures," she said, "and then a letter would come confirming God and his strength. I would be awakened to hope once again. Her persistence kept me 'in the faith.'"

60

Intercessory prayer empowers the witness.

As a result of the sewing course and Bible class the church women offered for the community women, they were invited to a country village to share the gospel with an enrollee's family and friends.

Thirty people had gathered when the seven church women arrived to share the gospel. "At the end when we asked who wanted to accept Jesus as Savior, all we got was blank stares," recalls missionary Mary Jo Stewart. "They had not understood. They did not know anything about God.

"The next week we decided to start at the beginning with a flannelgraph story of the creation. Each week we taught Bible stories which they loved and thought were beautiful. But each time as we asked who wanted to believe in Jesus, there was no response.

"Finally, I decided to act in a more positive spiritual manner. I wrote to several real pray-ers in the U.S. and asked them to pray for this group every Thursday at 3 PM.

"I had so much confidence in their prayers that I asked the bivocational pastor if he could get off work and go with us the next week. He managed to do so and declared en route to the village, 'We are going to see some results today. I just know it.'

"After we sang the usual hymns, the pastor explained John 3:16 very simply and asked how many wanted to accept Jesus. The first woman, then her husband, then nearly all the adults responded. We were so excited we forgot to count how many, but there were approximately eighteen professions of faith."

Intercessors can lift missionaries' burdens.

The missionary couple's oldest son was one of those fortunate enough to be accepted in an excellent, prestigious college. Returning to the United States from overseas, he made an excellent record the first semester. Then his grades began to drop and finally he withdrew before the term's end. His parents could not learn the reasons.

Arriving the next summer on furlough, they visited him and found him working in a fast-food place and still uncommunicative about his problems.

They settled in their home state a long distance from where the son lived. He moved and they lost contact.

"It was getting close to Christmas," the mother shared, "and I longed for him to spend Christmas with us. But we could not get in touch.

"I shared with several mission groups and asked them to pray with us about this. The first week of December while meeting with a mission prayer group I again asked for prayer. The leader stopped and prayed right then that we would hear from our son before the day was over.

"Two days later he cut his arm and two days after that he called! The next week he came home for two and a half weeks while he was recuperating. Since then we have been in touch."

"I have learned a precious truth about prayer," declares missionary Tom Thurman. "When our burdens get greater and the stress is heavier, people at home who are prayer partners sense this need and respond with extra prayer on our behalf.

"Last year was especially difficult for us," he admits. "Our youngest, David, eleven, went off to school out of the country for the first time. Gloria suffered much with arthritis. Converts returned to their former religion.

"Toward the end of the year we began to receive letters from persons who had been burdened to pray for us during the year."

Intercession strengthens the missionary.

A woman noted in a Christmas card to Mary Hazel Moon that her bravery had always been inspirational to her. Her father had died in an automobile accident and her sister had a stroke while she was overseas.

"I had peace at the time of the problems," she said, "but I never thought about being brave. Then I realized that one main reason I had peace at those times was because my Christian friends in my home church knew about the crises in my life before I did and they had had the opportunity to pray for me before I received the news."

Intercession blesses at both ends.

"When everyone saw us off at the airport, Mother was the only one who never shed a tear," recounts missionary Helen Hardeman. "She just cheered us on.

"When we left for language study I was six-and-a-half months pregnant. We got settled, started school, and located a doctor. On my first visit he told me the baby was going to be early and put me to bed.

"The next checkup he put me in the hospital that night. Nobody in the United States knew.

"We did not learn until five months later that when Mother had her devotional time that night she began to be uneasy for the first time. Worried and upset, she cried, prayed, and read her Bible till late in the night. Suddenly she felt a real peace that the same Lord who took care of us in the U.S. could surely take care of us overseas, too.

"Even later we learned a pastor's wife who was close to us waked in the middle of the night thinking of us, got up and prayed until she too had peace.

"The moment they both received peace happened to be the hour our baby was born!

The story from where I was is that I could speak no Spanish and the Lord sent a missionary nurse who had just completed another delivery. She stopped by to ask if I would like her to stay with me. She remained the whole time.

"That is when I became aware personally what intercessory prayer really means."

Intercession is ultimate method.

They had tried everything with the eight-year-old "holy terror." Sunday School teachers at Pine Street Church and workers at Oregon Hill Center located at the church had stretched their patience the second mile because of his problems.

His father had been in prison since the boy was three. His mother rebuffed discussion of his behavior, first by coolness and then by turning away. When his father was paroled, he acted worse.

Evelyn Berry, who with her husband, Bill, directs the center, enlisted her small prayer group's intercession for the parents to accept Jesus as Savior, for a job for the father, and for a change in the boy.

His behavior disrupted summer activities led by a visiting youth group from Ridge Church. He frustrated and defeated their goals. A member of the group was prevented by her nursing schedule from working actively with the children, but she contributed faithful praying, especially for the unruly boy.

Turning violent while drinking heavily, the father slashed his wife from throat to waist and was returned to prison. In the hospital near death, the mother was attended by the nurse from Ridge Church who also prayed for and lovingly shared Christ with her.

Upon recovery, the woman followed the nurse's suggestion to attend church and center activities and gradually began sharing her problems with the group. Not until Mrs. Berry spoke at Ridge Church did either she or the nurse discover the ways God had coordinated both their praying and ministering. It was then the nurse realized her patient was the mother of the incorrigible boy.

"He behaves like a different child," exclaims Evelyn. "We had tried everything under the sun. I know the Lord changed him in direct answer to prayer."

14
Prayer and God's Word

Personally I doubt there are any strong pray-ers who are not strong in the Bible also.

Communication with God is essential. It is not one-sided.

God speaks to us through his Word and his Holy Spirit. We speak to him through prayer.

Strong relationships are built on mutual sharing, on dialogue, not monologues. We must listen to God in order to know him.

If we spend more time with television, newspapers, books, and magazines than with the living, powerful, inspired Word of God, we will know more about the temporary world than about the eternal God. We may be well-informed, but we are not wise.

The secret of much unanswered prayer is "We are not listening to God's Word and therefore He is not listening to our petitions."[1]

Even though she'd been raised in a Christian home and had read the Bible all her life, missionary Yvonne Helton began to feel there was more Christ wanted to do in her life.

Being a readaholic she had worked in high school, college, and seminary libraries and admitted she probably spent more time reading than putting away books.

"If you had asked about my priorities, I would have said Bible reading first," she states. "But the time I spent in other things did not reflect that. So I decided to try an experiment for one month: to put away all other reading matter and read only the Bible."

Non-readaholics, she feels, would not appreciate how hard she found it and how often she was tempted to just glance at a book or take a peek at magazines and other boat mail from the U.S. "But I decided that was my time to really get to know Jesus Christ and to know him better.

"As I began reading through the Bible I felt like a child discovering it for the first time. The message seemed to have been written just for me. Each page had a special message.

"After reading 1,189 chapters I was at the end of the book and the end of the month. It was such an exciting experience I decided to try it again!"

This time she began a study of special topics, like the love of God, peace, faith, worship. "God began to speak to me and penetrate my life in some very special ways," she discloses. "I have had more opportunities and more ways to share Christ since then than I ever had before."

Deeper Bible study and spiritual hunger usually precede a deeper prayer life.

Reading the Bible through in a year, this year for the twentieth time, missionary Barbara Deal explains, "I have enjoyed my devotional time for many years. But I did not spend much time praying except with my husband, at prayer services, or in our family devotional.

"I began to pray that God would help me learn to spend more time in prayer, to be in his presence, to feel the power of his love and his Spirit." She describes a new practice of keeping a prayer notebook in connection with Bible study. "I cannot tell what a blessing this has been to me."

Deep Bible study is necessary to a deep prayer life.

The statement sounded like the modern philosophy of the "me-first" generation when I first read it:

"I saw more clearly than ever that the first great and primary business to which I ought to attend every day was to have my soul happy in the Lord."

But the language was old-timey and I discovered George Mueller wrote it in 1841. No self-centered, turned-inward mystic, he was one of the greatest men of prayer and practical Christian activists who ever lived.

"The first thing to be concerned about," he continued, "was not how much I might serve the Lord or how I might glorify the Lord, but how I might get my soul into a happy state, and how my inner man might be nourished."

He might work to convert sinners, strengthen believers, alleviate suffering, and try to express his faith as a true Christian, he wrote, but if he were not "happy in the Lord" and if not "nourished and strengthened" in his inner self day by day, he would not be doing it in a right spirit.

For ten years Mueller had given himself to prayer immediately after dressing in the morning until breakfast. The result was that his mind often wandered and he had problems concentrating for the first ten to thirty minutes before he could really begin to pray. He admitted he often spent fifteen minutes to an hour on his knees before he consciously "derived comfort, encouragement, humbling of soul, etc."

Then to his astonishment he discovered a point he had never

learned from a fellow Christian nor from any book or sermon. From the moment the Lord taught it to him it seemed clear and logical that "the first thing the child of God has to do morning by morning is to obtain food for his inner man."

Just as physical man is not able to work very long without food and since eating is one of the first things we do in the morning, so we should take food first for the inner man.

"What is the food for inner man?" he asks. "Not prayer, but the Word of God."

Mueller underscores the point that it is not just "the simple reading of the Word of God so that it only passes through our minds, just as water runs through a pipe." We should think about what we read, ponder it, and apply it to our hearts.

He began his new practice. After briefly asking the Lord's blessing on his Word, he began first to meditate on it, "searching into every verse to get blessing out of it," not to use in preaching but as "food" for his own soul.

He discovered the result to be almost invariably that after a very few minutes he had been led to confession or to thanksgiving or to intercession or to supplication. "Though I did not, as it were, give myself to prayer, but to meditation, yet it turned almost immediately more or less into prayer."

As he proceeded to the next words or verse, he would follow where the Word might lead into prayer for himself or for others. But he kept his purpose continually before himself: the purpose of his meditation was food for his own soul.

With only rare exceptions, by breakfast time he was "in a peaceful if not happy state of heart.

"My heart being nourished by the truth, being brought into experimental fellowship with God, I speak to my Father and to my Friend (vile though I am and unworthy of it) about the things that He has brought before me in His precious Word."

He read larger portions of the Bible after family prayer and during the day took more time especially for prayer.

Because of the immense spiritual profit and refreshment gained from this practice of twenty-six years, Mueller writes, "I affection-ately and solemnly beseech all my fellow believers to ponder this matter."[2]

Mueller's life proves the statement that "throughout the ages the Word has fashioned intercessors."[3]

Whatever deepens Bible study and prayer is worthwhile.
During two difficult beginning years on the mission field, missionary Roberta Fisher learned to turn to and depend on God through Scripture and prayer.

"I can sum it all up," she declares, "in the words of the psalmist: 'It is good for me that I have been afflicted; that I might learn thy statutes' (Ps. 119:71), and also 'Unless thy law had been my delights, I should then have perished in mine affliction'" (v. 92).

15
Prayer and the Promises

Jesus says his followers may ask for *anything*. Does he really mean just that? What about the unlimited promises or the blank checks, as they are called?

Jesus began his public ministry with the Sermon on the Mount and closed it with his final counsel in John, chapters 14-16. He began by preaching to a crowd and ended by teaching a small group, eleven apostles.

In the beginning he was speaking to new followers, explaining that God is a loving, giving Heavenly Father who wants a personal relationship with them and who invites them to bring him their personal needs.

At the end he was turning over his kingdom's operation to seasoned disciples, outlining prayer as the way they would carry out the impossible task committed to them.

At the first he encouraged his followers in a simple, childlike trust. At the last he challenged them to a bold faith in God's power to change and overcome the world.

"You are no longer employees who do not know what the employer is doing," Jesus says in effect, "but you are now friends and partners in whom I am confiding and to whom I am committing my work. My Father has been carrying out his work through me. Now he will continue it through you."

Listen to the sweeping promises he made:

"Whatsoever ye shall ask in my name, that will I do" (John 14:13).

"If you ask anything in my name, I will do it" (John 14:14).

"If ye abide in me, and my words abide in you, ye shall ask what you will, and it shall be done unto you" (John 15:7).

"Whatsoever you shall ask of the Father in my name, he may give it you" (John 15:16).

"Whatsoever ye shall ask the Father in my name, he will give it you" (John 16:23).

"Ask, and ye shall receive, that your joy may be full" (John 16:24).

These have been called unlimited promises. And they are, in the sense that what God can accomplish through our praying is beyond all limits of what we can think, dream, or imagine.

In another sense they are limited. The limits are asking for what Jesus would ask in that situation (in his name) and for God's glory.

Study the passages and see that the promises have conditions. They are tied to our being vitally connected to Jesus (abiding in him), his words living in our hearts, keeping his commandments so as to live in the consciousness of his love, being fruitful and passing on the message, and finding peace and victory while facing tribulation and distress.

"How many a believer has read these over with joy and hope," exclaims Andrew Murray, "and in deep earnestness of soul has sought to plead them for his own need. And he has come out disappointed."[1]

The simple reason, Murray explains, is that he has taken the promise out of context. "The Lord gave the wonderful promise of the free use of His Name with the Father in connection with the *doing of His works.* It is the disciple who gives himself wholly to live for Jesus' work and kingdom, for his will and honour, to whom the power will come to appropriate the promise." The person who would use the promise for his own special desire, says Murray, will be disappointed because he is trying to "make Jesus the servant of his own comfort."

But to the one who aspires to pray the prayer of faith because he needs it for the Master's work and "because he has made himself the servant of his Lord's interest," the Lord will teach and strengthen him in praying. "Prayer not only teaches and strengthens to work: work teaches and strengthens to pray.

"As you give yourself entirely to God for His work," he predicts, "you will feel that nothing less than these great promises are what you need, that nothing less is what you may most confidently expect."

A friend of mine has a joint bank account with her elderly parents. The money belongs to her parents. None of it was earned or rightfully belongs to my friend. Yet she may freely write checks on this account.

Her only reason for writing the checks is to take care of her parents' business. She pays their monthly bills and keeps track of their expenditures. She never writes a check to herself unless it is money legitimately owed her for expenses incurred in overseeing their affairs.

I do not know all the reasons this daughter was chosen to handle their business instead of the other grown children. Perhaps she had maintained a closer relationship through the years. But one reason I know. She is honest.

She has proven her honesty and integrity through the years in the way she has handled her own affairs and the responsibilities they have given her. They know she will not appropriate one dollar for her personal use. She has shown she is interested solely in their welfare and the success of their business undertakings.

This, to me, is a modern parable of prayer. Though not perfect in every detail, because God is the parent, the banker, the auditor, etc., it gives one main lesson of a parable.

Our Father has chosen to take us into his "business." If we willingly and responsibly accept assignments, he discovers he can trust us. If we grow and mature spiritually, his kingdom becomes our business, too. We want it to thrive. It is more important to us than anything else. We want only what he wants.

He gives us blank checks to use in his affairs that may be filled in for whatever amount is needed. They are signed by his Son, our Elder Brother. We will not use them for our own selfish pleasures, conveniences, or ambitions. They are only for furthering his enterprise.

Working for him, we have personal "expenses" (needs) that he will underwrite. He will approve them because they are not self-centered requests, but necessary, legitimate ones for equipping us to do his work.

If we feel something is in his interest but are not sure, we need to confer with him and get his approval before writing the check.

"In no case," writes R. A. Torrey, "does real faith come by simply determining that you are going to get the thing that you want to get. If we are to have real faith, we must study the Word of God and find out what is promised, then simply believe the promises of God."

16
Prayer and the Holy Spirit

Jeanie Ledbetter, a fourteen-year-old MK at the time, was feeling worse. For several days she had tried her mother's remedy for everything, "take an aspirin and lie down."

"Sunday before Thanksgiving," Ethel recalls, "I realized our daughter was really ill. My husband went to a nearby Baptist church to find our doctor."

After admission to the hospital and many tests and medication for three days, Jeanie was diagnosed as having a combination of illnesses. The doctor seemed worried about her high fever, fast heartbeat, and growing weakness as stomach pains increased.

Local hospital regulations allowed Ethel to stay with her day and night, "but I felt completely helpless. She was in severe pain Wednesday night. The nurses assured me she had been given all the medication she was allowed.

"I was rubbing her stomach between 1 and 2 AM when suddenly I thought, *Jeanie is going to die! The Lord may take her tonight!* Instantly I became ill and groped my way to a couch to keep from passing out. As I lay there I prayed. When I was able to return to her bedside, she was sleeping peacefully."

That morning was Thanksgiving—on the calendar as well as in Mike's and Ethel's hearts. "The medicine is finally taking effect," the doctor declared, smiling at Ethel. "We both knew it was the Lord working." Jeanie was discharged two days later.

About two weeks afterward a letter arrived from a friend in Calvary Baptist Church, Winston-Salem, North Carolina.

"Betty shared that she had been burdened for us recently. It seemed the Lord was bringing our names often to her for prayer. This continued several days. Then, one night she felt the Lord woke her and immediately she knew she must pray for us. Getting out of bed on her knees, she told the Lord she could not imagine what was the matter, but asked that he meet our needs, whatever they might be. She was writing to ask if we had had a special need about 2 AM Thanksgiving morning!

"Praise God for his servants," Ethel exclaims, "whom he can wake in the middle of the night to pray."

The Holy Spirit prompts praying.

The Holy Spirit is not only our Teacher in praying, but he guides, empowers, and even prays through us. All he needs is access.

Many of us give up meaningful praying because we try it in our own strength. Nothing is more discouraging and exhausting than trying to do spiritual work with human power.

"Following after the Holy Spirit leads to life and peace, but following after the old nature leads to death, because the old sinful nature within us is against God. It never did obey God's laws and it never will" (Rom. 8:6-7, TLB). That is why we have to die to our own sinful desires and ambitions daily in order to follow Jesus (Luke 9:23).

The Holy Spirit comes to dwell in any person who accepts Jesus Christ as Savior, but often the new believer is not aware or does not experience the truth of this doctrine. Others of us may know, but allow him only as guest, not as master. We are to keep on "being filled" and controlled by him (Eph. 5:18).

The Spirit's main and first function is to reveal and glorify Jesus Christ.

Andrew Murray maintains that the Holy Spirit's first and greatest work is to reveal the ascended Christ to believers so they may know him personally.[1]

He wants us to understand the truth "that the many references through the New Testament[2] to Christ in you, you in Christ, Christ our life and abiding in Christ, are literal, actual, blessed fact—not figures of speech."[3]

Listen to Charles Trumbull's testimony: "At last I realized that Jesus Christ was actually and literally within me. And even more than that: that He constituted my very life, taking me into union with Himself—my body, mind, and spirit—while I still had my own identity and free will and full moral responsibility.

"Was this not better than having Him as a helper, or even than having Him as an external Savior: to have Him, Jesus Christ, God the Son, as my very own life?

"It meant that I need never again ask Him to help me as though He were one and I another; but rather simply to do His work, His will, in me and with me and through me. My body was His, my mind His, my will His, my spirit His; and not merely His, but literally a part of Him. What He asked me to recognize was, 'I have

73

been crucified with Christ, and it is no longer I that live, but Christ liveth in me.'"[4]

The Holy Spirit convicts of sin.

"I could not have gone back to the mission field if I had not had a renewal experience on furlough," admits missionary C. R. (Buck) Smith.

"I had ill will and hard feelings toward a fellow missionary. While on retreat with a young people's group, we met to pray and renew our vows to the Lord at a New Year's Eve service. God used the Scripture about washing one another's feet as he had done. I realized I wasn't in a position to wash my brother's feet because I had pride and unforgiveness.

"The Holy Spirit is like a bright light searching out all the darkness and sin in our lives, spotlighting it, and telling us what to confess. We as Christians need to live transparent lives."

After receiving personal forgiveness, Buck knew he needed to tell his brother in Christ. "He did not realize I had the ill will but it was a very meaningful experience for us both. I believe the staying power of the gospel is found in the forgiveness through Jesus Christ."

The Holy Spirit initiates world missions (Acts 1:8).

"The more we grow in maturity the better we understand that the executive of all Christian work is the Holy Spirit," write missionaries Amelio and Lidia Giannetta.

"We missionaries, conventions, agencies, churches, pastors, and church members are only instruments. To be used in this ministry, no matter who and where we are, we must fit in his plan and obey his call. He calls missionaries, pastors, evangelists, and laymen for specific jobs and for a specific time. Likewise he calls prayer intercessors for specific projects and for a determined period, because the ministry of intercession in his strategy is just as vital as that of sower or reaper.

"Just as the Holy Spirit, the omniscient coordinator of all

Christian work, has called us here he will call some of you to be prayer intercessors for the work he sent us to do."

The Holy Spirit empowers.

Having internal problems, the church had postponed revival meetings twice and the pastor almost called missionary Amelio Giannetta to cancel the third scheduled meeting.

A half-empty auditorium, many absent leaders, no visitors, and a cold spiritual atmosphere discouraged Giannetta the first two evenings. But he waited for the Lord, clinging to the verse, "The battle is not yours, but God's" (2 Chron. 20:15).

A group of older teenagers, who were professing agnostics and included the pastor's son, Andrea, kept coming. Giannetta had witnessed and written to Andrea for two-and-a-half years since first meeting him. "Andrea is too proud," his father said. "It will take years for him to surrender."

The last day Andrea came forward sobbing as soon as the invitation was given. At the end of the service the front of the church was full of young people. "We closed the five-day meeting with fourteen baptisms and eleven more professions of faith."

The Holy Spirit is the Master-Prayer.

"We cannot even pray correctly without the guidance of the Holy Spirit," declares missionary Ruthie Baggett.

The misconceptions we get are sometimes compounded by changes in English. Formerly when I read that "the Spirit also helpeth our infirmities . . . maketh intercession for us with groanings which cannot be uttered" (Rom. 8:26), I interpreted that to mean experiences of great pain or grief. Somehow I thought we prayed about normal things and the Holy Spirit took over in a crisis when we could not express our feelings.

Regardless of the language, my concept was still the carnal, human attitude that I will take care of everything, except what I cannot handle. Then I will call on God.

Listen to a clearer statement: "And in the same way—by our

faith—the Holy Spirit helps us with our daily problems and in our praying. For we don't even know what we should pray for, nor how to pray as we should; but the Holy Spirit prays for us with such feeling that it cannot be expressed in words. And the Father who knows all hearts knows, of course, what the spirit is saying as he pleads for us in harmony with God's own will" (Rom. 8:26-27, TLB).

How liberating to learn that it meant what Gordon explains: "It is our infirmity that we do not know how to pray *as we ought*. There is willingness and eagerness too. No bother there. But a lack of knowledge. We don't know how. But the Spirit knows how. He is the Master-prayor. He knows God's will perfectly. He knows what best to be praying under all circumstances. And He is within you and me. He is there as a prayer-spirit. He prompts us to pray."[5]

He is called both the spirit of prayer (Zech. 12:10, TEV), and the Comforter (John 14:16). His very names should convince us it is his delight to teach us to pray. All he needs is our surrender. He must overcome us to bless us.

If we find it a burden and hardship to learn, it is most likely we are hampered by misconceptions, self-effort, unconfessed sin, or failure to submit to him.

The Holy Spirit gives individual guidance and blessing.

Not only does he equip us with "gifts" for service,[6] but he produces "fruit" (Gal. 5:22-23)—attitudes of thought and virtues of life expressing God's nature—that we receive through prayer.

Communist revolutionaries spread out over the city of Jakarta to seize strategic spots, including power and communication centers, and to capture the Indonesian army's top commanding generals.

Communication and traffic to the outside world were cut off. Mail was halted and telephone lines were unavailable for days. Only ominous news reached missionaries' families in the U.S. There were rumors of eliminating religious leaders, including missionaries, when the Communists were fully in control.

Kate O'Brien called relatives to intense prayer as she waited for news from her son, William R. O'Brien, then a missionary in

Central Java. As she fasted and prayed, the Lord gave her a Scripture passage which comforted and promised God's sustaining presence: "Fear not: for I have redeemed thee, I have called thee by thy name; thou art mine. When thou passest through the waters, I will be with thee; and through the rivers, they shall not overflow thee: when thou walkest through the fire, thou shalt not be burned; neither shall the flame kindle upon thee. For I am the Lord thy God, the Holy One of Israel" (Isa. 43:1-3).

Eventually the coup was crushed and the Communists were purged. Communication was restored. God had protected the missionaries.

When he and his family came on furlough, O'Brien related, "During those difficult days in Indonesia, a passage from Isaiah gave us security and comfort; "When thou passest through the waters, I will be with thee!"

"Who needs cables, telephones, or even letters," asks Mrs. O'Brien, "when God can strengthen loved ones a world apart with the identical message from himself?"

17
Prayer and Dependence

You and I were meant to be completely dependent on God. This is just the opposite of what our human nature and our culture tell us.

In our American culture parents are to help a child become independent, giving him more and more responsibility until he can make his own decisions and live his own life.

This is reinforced by our cultural sayings like "Stand on your own two feet," "Make it on your own," "Every tub sits on its own bottom," and "A parent's function is to give roots and wings." As a poet expressed it, "I am the master of my fate;/I am the captain of my soul."[1]

In relationship to parents, we must become independent. In

relationship to God, nothing could be further from the truth. Norman Grubb is quoted as saying, "Any independence man has is an illusion."

There is no way we can independently determine what will happen to us in life. Jeremiah knew this truth: "Lord, I know that no one is the master of his own destiny. No person has control over his own life" (Jer. 10:23, TEV). Nor were we ever meant to be independent spiritually.

The most important lesson I have learned since becoming a Christian is what I call "dying to self" or "complete dependence." It has also been the most liberating.

Some call it "the crucified life" or "giving up self" or "coming to the end of yourself" or "living by faith" or "living by the life of Another." Whatever it's called, it begins with helplessness.

It is based on Jesus' saying, "If anyone wants to follow in my footsteps, he must give up all right to himself, carry his cross [his instrument of death] every day and keep close behind me" (Luke 9:23, Phillips).[2]

Inseparable from the idea of helplessness is the knowledge that Jesus lives in us by means of his Spirit and lives the Christian life through us. We cannot do it, but he can! "Christ [is] in you, the hope of glory" (Col. 1:27), or the hope of your becoming all God wants you to be.

Just as I could not save myself, so I cannot live the Christian life. Just as I asked him to save me, so I must ask him to live the Christian life through me.

My best was not good enough to save me and so I trust in Jesus for salvation. My best is not good enough to live the impossible Christian life and so I trust him to do it for me and through me. God does not want my best; it is not good enough. He does not want me to try harder; he wants me to die—to get out of the way and let him do it through me.

I live this new life by faith. The Bible speaks of "the obedience of faith." The opposite of that is the "disobedience of self-effort," which cannot please God. In fact, it displeases him. It keeps us from receiving all the blessings he has for us through faith.[3]

Transaction of dependence.

"It was my experience on the mission field," declares Martha Franks, missionary veteran of forty-one years in China and Taiwan, "that you come to the end of yourself and let the Lord be all and in all, *everything,* or you go under or (I hate to say it) you stay on as a second-rate missionary.

"I will praise the Lord throughout all eternity that he took me to the mission field to discover what I might not have learned if I had not come face to face with situations where I could not cope. I saw that either you come to the place of total commitment and dependency on the Lord for everything or you miss the point!"

Can a person serve the Lord without this kind of dependence? we ask.

"Oh, yes," Miss Franks answers. "People can serve the Lord without that kind of relationship to him. In fact, many do. I don't think there are many people who find it."

Why is that?

"Self. We have such exalted opinions of ourselves. And we are ignorant. We don't know there is something better. But there is!"

What do you call this experience? The deeper Christian life? Dying to self?

"Yes. Fullness of the Holy Spirit. Total surrender. It has many names. They all mean the same thing."

How do you experience it?

"Well, I had to realize that I needed more than I had. I thought I had it all. In fact, I thought the Chinese were real lucky to get me. But in my first encounter with two pagan, rural Chinese women I thought if I just witnessed to them they were going to fall down converted. But they didn't. And it was a shock.

"That was in my second year, the hard year. I said, 'Now, Lord, if it's going to be like this I want to go home to my mama.'

"But one of the women in our station knew about this coming to the end of self and I saw that she was different. Through reading books she gave me, I learned about it. I came to see that I must come to the end of myself, which is not easy to do. But I did. Some have an emotional experience and some don't. I did. I think the

Lord knew I needed it because I had really been in despair. I was ready to give up.

"Some have no emotion. But I am inclined to think a definite transaction is necessary. The first thing is to realize your need and then to understand there must be death to self—being alive to God.

"One woman I know just said, 'Lord, I have been on the throne of my heart. I have been calling the shots, I have been making the plans. I have had the reins in my hands. Now by faith I get off the throne of my heart and I put you there. As of now, I am under new management. You are the manager.'"

Dependence in prayer.

A well-known minister, able and devoted, wrote Andrew Murray saying it discouraged him to hear too much about the "strenuous exertion and all the time, trouble, and endless effort it will cost" to prepare for a life of prayer. He had heard it often, he said, tried it again and again, and had always been sadly disappointed.

Murray replied that he had never in any conference or sermon mentioned exertion or struggle, "because I am convinced that our efforts are futile unless we first learn to abide in Christ by a simple faith."

The minister continued that the message he needed to hear was that we should see that our relationship to our living Savior is what it should be. Further, he said, we should "live in His presence, rejoice in His love, rest in Him." Murray agreed, *if* a proper relationship were *rightly* understood.

We should not think we are in a right relationship, Murray feels, "while the sin of prayerlessness has power over us." If we understand that a right relationship to the Lord Jesus will include both the desire and the power to pray, then we can rejoice and rest in him.

The first step, he explains, is not to struggle and strive in our own strength but to cast ourselves at the feet of Jesus and wait on him in the sure confidence he is with us and works in us.

The second step *is* a struggle, but it is the striving of *faith*.

Murray continues, "The Scripture speaks of 'the good fight of faith' . . . which springs from and is carried on by faith. . . . Strive in prayer; let faith fill your heart—so you will be strong in the Lord and in the power of His might."

The second step only comes after the first. If we do not come to Jesus in helplessness and dependence, just as we did for salvation, then we will never persevere in the second phase of prayer.

Those of us who condemn ourselves for our prayerlessness, our many broken resolutions and futile attempts to pray faithfully have fixed our eyes on ourselves, not the Lord Jesus, according to Murray.

We need to tell the Lord how it is. "Lord, My heart is far from you. I do not feel like praying. I do not know how to pray. I cannot seem to persevere. I know I should pray for your work in the world but I have no desire. But I know you want me to and I look to you. I cannot help myself. I believe you will. Help me, I pray."

Murray says when we pray like that the Lord Jesus in his tender love is looking down and saying, "'You cannot pray. . . . Only believe that I am ready to help you in prayer. . . . Just as I will cleanse you from all other sins, so also will I deliver you from the sin of prayerlessness—only do not seek the victory in your own strength. Bow before Me as one who expects everything from his Saviour. . . . Be assured of this—I will teach you how to pray.'"[4]

18
Prayer and Faith

The Christian life is a life of faith—of complete confidence in a loving God and obedience to his will. Or it should be!

The words translated as *faith* and *believe* are used almost five hundred times in the New Testament. They carry the idea, not of believing merely with your mind, but of trusting in, relying on, and cleaving to God.

The essence of faith is believing God.

The essence of sin is not believing God (John 16:9).

Faith is believing that God, whom we cannot see, exists and that he will reveal himself to those of us who seek him. By faith we receive his approval and please him. Without it we cannot possibly do so (Heb. 11:6).

Faith is believing what he says to us through his written Word, the Bible, and through his living Word, Jesus Christ his Son. Faith is believing that what he says is true, that what he promises is sure.

Faith believes that the spiritual, unseen world is more real than this present physical one which will pass away. Therefore, it believes that living and working for God's rule here on earth is the most important and lasting thing we can do (1 John 2:15-17).

We may pray in faith for anything the Bible reveals as God's will. We may pray in faith for any and every person to be saved because "The Lord . . . is not willing that any should perish, but that all should come to repentance" (2 Pet. 3:9).

We may pray in faith for countries to open and remain accessible to the gospel since Jesus commanded, "Go therefore and make disciples of all the nations" (Matt. 28:19, NASB).

We may pray in faith for a land to become responsive to the Lord Christ, because the Father God says to his Son, "Ask and I will give you all the nations; the whole earth will be yours" (Ps. 2:8, TEV).

"Have faith in God," Jesus instructed. "I tell you: When you pray and ask for something, believe that you have received it, and you will be given whatever you ask for" (Mark 11:22,24, TEV).

Our faith must be in God. Not in our prayers. Not in our faith. Not in someone else's prayers in our behalf. Not in the urgency of our need. Not in our worthiness or lack of it. Not in our feelings. But in God.

Often we are tempted as missionary Jo Scales expresses it: "I must confess I felt my prayer life had been pretty much a series of victories. All the really big things I had prayed for, the Lord had answered in the affirmative. I felt sure the prayers that had not received an immediate yes would eventually be granted. God had never given me a flat no on the big ones. I felt I was a pretty successful pray-er."

Subsequently she joined in a prayer vigil for the injured son of missionaries. His younger brother had been run over by a friend's car and died a few years earlier. Now he lay in critical condition in the hospital, victim of the same type accident. One woman persuaded the group, after confessing their sins so as not to block the Holy Spirit's power, to ask for the boy's life.

"We demanded his life. That night he died." The tears she shed were not only of grief, but also disappointment and disillusionment. Finally, God's peace and love took over.

Why did God allow this to happen? "I don't know," she admits. "But I believe praying is an act of faith—we believe God will answer as he sees best for us. To expect to get everything we want is as foolish as thinking we know more than God does."

We started by saying that the Christian life is a life of faith. But few of us really believe or practice it. If we did, we would know that consistent and constant prayer is an absolute necessity, not an option.

We are brought into right standing with God (Rom. 3:28) and become his children by faith (Gal. 3:26). God counts our faith as righteousness and it gives us access to him (Rom 5:2). We are saved by faith (Eph. 2:8). We receive the Holy Spirit by faith (Gal. 3:5).

We are to live (Rom. 1:17), stand (Rom. 11:20), walk (2 Cor. 5:7), obey (Rom. 16:26), and fight (1 Tim. 6:12) by faith. We inherit God's promises (Heb. 6:12) and are shielded from Satan's attacks by faith (Eph. 6:16). We are to pursue faith (2 Tim. 2:22) and to prove by our works that we have it (Jas. 2:18). Anything not based on faith is sin (Rom. 14:23).

The testing of our faith brings honor, praise, and glory to Jesus Christ (1 Pet. 1:7). Faith is produced by the Holy Spirit (Gal. 5:22). By faith we can conquer the world (1 John 5:4). Jesus began and will complete our pilgrimage of faith (Heb. 12:2).

There are some things God does regardless of our faith, or lack of it. There are others in which he has chosen to limit himself according to the measure of our faith.

Matthew tells us, "Because they did not have faith, he did not perform many miracles there (Matt. 13:58, TEV). Mark goes even further, recording, "He was not able to perform any miracles there, except that he placed his hands on a few sick people and healed them. He was greatly surprised, because the people did not have faith" (Mark 6:5-6, TEV). Perhaps the Lord cannot do mighty miracles in, for, or through us and our praying because we do not have faith.

One of the biggest blocks to our faith is thinking of God in human terms. We try to make him like ourselves and give him our limitations. We think of him as bigger and better than ourselves, stronger and smarter than Superman. Yet still we visualize him as a sort of super creature.

"I am God, and not man, the Holy One in your midst," says our Creator (Hos. 11:9, RSV). "Is anything too hard for the Lord?" (Gen. 18:14). "Nothing," we answer in awe.

Few of us feel we have enough faith when we pray. Since believing and praying go together, how do we get more faith?

First, it doesn't take much. A *little* faith goes a long way. If we have faith as big as a mustard seed, Jesus taught, we can tell a mountain to move and it will (Matt. 17:20). Mustard seeds are some of the smallest seeds around, but that's all we need to "do *anything!*"

Second, we can ask for more. We pray with the disciples, "Lord, increase our faith" (Luke 17:5). Or with the desperate father, "I do have faith, but not enough. Help me have more" (Mark 9:24, TEV).

Third, faith is awakened by God's Word. "Faith cometh by hearing, and hearing by the word of God" (Rom. 10:17). We have quoted this basic passage about missions so often and glibly that we have overlooked some of its meaning. Yes, it means that lost persons hearing the gospel can receive saving faith through the message. Therefore, we are responsible to send and take it.

84

But it also means that our faith is stirred up by reading, hearing, memorizing, meditating on, and "living in" the Scriptures.

Fourth, thanking God for specific blessings and answers to prayer can strengthen our faith. "Doubtless the reason so many have so little faith when they pray," writes R. A. Torrey, "is because they take so little time to meditate upon and thank God for blessings already received. As one meditates upon the answer to prayers already granted, faith waxes bolder and bolder, and we come to feel in the very depths of our souls that there is nothing too hard for the Lord."[1]

As we compare how little thought, strength, and time we put into thanksgiving compared to "the wondrous goodness of God" toward us, Torrey says, this should cause us to humble ourselves and confess our sin before God.[2]

George Mueller gives three more suggestions for increasing one's faith. Fifth, maintain an upright life and a good conscience. (Heb. 10:22). Sixth, do not shrink from opportunities where your faith may be tried (1 Pet. 1:7). Seventh, do not work a deliverance for yourself when the hour of trial comes (Dan. 3:16-18).

19
Prayer and Obedience

If faith is anything, it is obedience. Believing is active, not passive. Read the "faith" chapter, Hebrews 11, and see all the actions, attitudes, and accomplishments produced by faith.

Paul speaks of the "obedience of faith" (Rom. 16:26). My favorite translations are "obedience inspired by faith" (Williams), and the "obedience that springs from faith" (Rom. 1:5, Weymouth).[1]

An old definition of faith is "stepping out when you do not see anything to step on." But faith has many definitions and "faces." Among others, faith is being convinced that God is, that he is spirit, and that it's worth our time to seek him with our whole heart.

Faith is praying instead of doing it on our own.

Interesting! In the world experience produces self-confidence, but in the Kingdom it brings dependence! The more experience and maturity Christians have, the less we venture on our own without God.

Serving as missionaries to South Vietnam for sixteen of their twenty-eight years under appointment, Bob and Ida Davis lived six years in Hue next to the North Vietnam border. Each family member kept a suitcase packed in case of sudden evacuation.

Bob said, "I am more dependent on prayer now than ever, and more consistent. I have more faith in God's care and provision."

Faith is resting in prayer when you worry and fear the worst.

A missionary mother waked in the middle of the night, deeply disturbed about her daughter's approaching marriage to a young man who was morally upright but not committed to the Lord and the church. She prayed, thinking about the daughter back in the United States and wishing it was less difficult to communicate from Africa.

"The Lord lovingly said to me, 'Go back to sleep. It's all right.'" The next evening the daughter called saying she had broken her engagement. A few weeks later she determined the Lord's purpose for her life and entered seminary. "It has been a joyous experience," exclaims her mother, "to see her marry a fine seminary student."

Faith is waiting in prayer when you'd rather be doing.

Missionary Elizabeth Hale left Shanghai in 1943 because she was needed at home. Six years later, when she was free to return, China was closed.

"The longing to 'tell the old, old story of Jesus and his love to those who had never heard' had filled my heart since I was nine," Elizabeth declared. "But I was told to wait. I accepted it and was filled with peace." She ministered to ill loved ones while she waited. "When the waiting was over, the joy I felt in being sent to Malaysia was greater than ever."

Faith is persisting in prayer when you would rather quit.

Dottie and Herman Hayes evacuated South Vietnam with other missionaries in 1975 when Communist forces took over. While Herman joined the other male missionaries to minister at the refugee receiving center on Guam, Dottie refugeed in a nearby country. As she prayed she faced her grief at losing her chosen country, people, and work.

"I thought I could never again learn another language, accept a new people, culture, and land," she recalls. "God gave me the beautiful Scripture, Isaiah 43:18-19, which turned my life around to the point I was willing to be available once again as he began that 'new thing' in my life. Soon after, we were on our way to Indonesia. Our visas were granted during our birthday times (August 27 and September 2)." (Southern Baptists publish a prayer calendar, listing missionaries on their birthday. So there are many people praying for missionaries on their birthday.)

Faith is following when an impression is all you have.

University Church in Beirut, Lebanon, needed desperately to find new quarters. Besides exorbitant rent, the old, two-story villa was freezing cold and considered unsafe. Some rooms had been closed because large slabs of ceiling plaster had fallen.

Returning from furlough, missionaries Bill and Evelyn Trimble resumed the unsuccessful search begun by the Charles Arringtons who preceded them. Combing the area of the city where the church ministered to foreigners and college students produced absolutely nothing. Apartments were scarce, too small for church use, and owned by landlords who would not rent to an evangelical congregation.

Church people and others were praying. As pastor, Bill felt the burden more than others. One morning in his study he laid the church's need before the Lord. The answer was "as clear as if I had heard it audibly or received a telegram." The new location was to be on Jeanne d'Arc Street between Bliss and Hamra Streets. He told no one except his wife.

Excitedly they scoured both sides of the street. Nothing turned up. But Bill knew God had reserved a place for their church in those few city blocks.

Stopping in a curio shop they explained their mission to the owner, a longtime acquaintance. He knew of nothing. "But, wait," he remembered, "there's a vacant place upstairs in this building." It had been a night club. Closed by police a year earlier because a man was killed in a fight, it was in terrible condition. But it was the place!

The church people shoveled and removed refuse, renovated, and remodeled. In an ideal location near American University, the area had a spacious auditorium and nine classrooms. It turned into the most worshipful and practical home the church could have imagined. And at less than half the rent they had been paying!

Faith is trying something new with no guarantees it will succeed.

"I have gone through the painful process of starting a new and different type work in a pioneer area," states missionary Becky Manferd. "Several have prayed for me and for the Lord's will in my work. It is difficult to start something new when few are as excited and convinced as you that it's really going to work. When I finally learned to leave it *all* in his hands, he has worked miracles."

With no church nearby, the mission purchased a small house next to the Manferd's mission residence in a middle-class neighborhood. Becky started an outreach ministry based on crafts, cooking, English, and exercise classes.

In the last five years she has given out more than five hundred Bibles to non-Christian neighbors. She conducts a Bible study for women, plus having countless opportunities to witness and counsel.

Faith is changing when the familiar is more secure.

To meet a critical need, Walter and Charlean Moore were asked to transfer to a mission hospital in Ghana rather than returning to their beloved Nigeria. "We were already facing the adjustment of returning for the first time without *any* of our family," they confided.

The decision meant leaving behind their mission family, their national brothers and sisters, the language they had struggled to learn, and the medical type work Dr. Moore had waited twenty years to do. "Only prayer made us able to do it and the rewards have been great."

Faith is action, working actively together with him.

Praying faith actively seeks openings to serve God, rather than expecting him to use someone else or to knock us down with opportunities.

"My most meaningful experiences in prayer," missionary Barbara Cole points out, "have come after praying that the Lord would provide opportunites to share Christ with certain individuals. In every case where I prayed this, I watched the Lord open the way."

Faith always obeys, whatever it may require.

During a mission emphasis in chapel at Southwestern Seminary, Walter Hunt was praying for any who should surrender to the invitation for missionaries. Bothered that most of those responding were young women, he thought a little impatiently, *Where are the men?* As the Lord reminded him he was a man and could answer his own question, as well as his prayer, he told the Lord he would go.

Faith is accepting prayer's answer before it comes.

In April 1977, Dr. and Mrs. Sam Cannata and their three children were arrested by government officials on serious charges and taken to the capital city from the interior where they served as medical missionaries. Ginny and the children were released the next day. Sam remained under detention. Though innocent, he knew the circumstantial evidence was incriminating and the suspicion of espionage was grave.

News was relayed to the U.S. and Christians began to pray. Gradually the spiritual trauma and depression began to lift as the Lord led Sam to see spiritual truths he had never seen. At the same time God also opened avenues of witness to the police and guards where he was imprisoned. "In short," Sam believes, "God was performing the miracle of Romans 8:28—taking a seemingly terrible situation and working it out for good."

Thirteen days later a cable from a San Antonio church promised a day of prayer for him. The next day the church and missionaries locally decided to start a prayer chain and pray until his release.

"I cannot describe the feeling that came over me," Sam exclaims. "With the new spiritual truths I had learned about prayer and the body of Christ, I felt in reality I was already released. God had moved his people, the body of Christ, to ask for my release and he is committed to honor the requests made in the powerful name of Jesus. I did not actually walk out of custody until three days later but, so far as I was concerned, the transaction was done when the church in concerted effort began to pray specifically. I'm convinced that these kinds of miracles can happen regularly when the church in harmony prays for specific things."

The writer of Hebrews cites persons who changed the shape of the world while considering themselves only foreigners and refugees in this life. They conquered kingdoms, endured unbelievable suffering and hardship, and performed tremendous acts of good because of faith (Heb. 11:13,33-38).

God, the Scripture says, is not ashamed of their kind (Heb. 11:16).

20
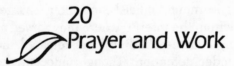Prayer and Work

When we pray, we work for God.
When we pray, we work with God.

Jesus tells several parables about servants or stewards in which the master assigns them tasks or makes them overseers in his business affairs.[1] He tells us that as we are concerned about his kingdom, our needs will be met, and, not to worry because he is pleased to give us his kingdom (Luke 12:32).

Paul points out that "we are labourers together with God" (1 Cor. 3:9). We work with each other and we work with God. We are partners in his business.

When we pray for God's missionaries, we share in their work. As missionary Ross Fryer wrote an intercessor, "You know that together we are participating in the work of our Lord's kingdom." We share in the work and in the rewards.

God's will is that all men be saved. The first and most important way to accomplish it is to pray for them.

"I exhort therefore, that, first of all," writes Paul, "supplications, prayers, intercessions, and giving of thanks be made for all men. . . . This is good and acceptable in the sight of God our Savior, who will have all men to be saved, and to come unto the knowledge of the truth" (1 Tim. 2:1,3-4).

Jesus gives us the general petition in the Model Prayer to pray for God's kingdom to come and his will be done in the hearts of men. He expects us to translate it into specific requests for persons, churches, mission causes, and nations that we know.

Prayer precedes any real work for God.

Many of us who have served God in any way have felt taking much time to pray held us up from "getting on with" the important work we needed to do for the Lord. As activists, we often do not consider prayer to be practical. Actually, nothing could be further from the truth.

God can order our priorities, eliminate exhausting self-effort, and give wisdom for decisions we cannot make through human understanding. From personal experience I have learned he can save me time, frustration, and confusion. When I let him, he will substitute his wise, best plans for my good ideas.

"I stopped 'working' for God," says missionary Gena Hampton, "and began letting him direct my life." Working in the publications ministry, missionary Aliene Hunt testifies, "I've learned to ask for God's direction in my work rather than ask his blessings on my already-prepared manuscript. It is a thrill to get his directions, or what I call my 'marching orders' every day."

Prayer provides needs in God's work.

During the current financial crunch, Mildred McWhorter de-clares she has witnessed more answers to pray in the last twelve months than in the nineteen years she has been associated as director of Baptist mission centers in Houston.

"Before, we had finance committees and budget funds to fall back on, but when the money hasn't come in from the churches, we have had to depend on the Lord.

"When we got to our last ounce of strength, with no funds coming in and no money to pay staff, the Lord sent funds and food from people we don't even know and have never heard of. We have not asked for funds. We have not sent out publicity. We have done nothing but pray! God has sent volunteers and provisions. He has put the pieces together. I have just stood back and watched.

"I can't even tell how fantastic it's been. So many unbelievable things have happened my own mother is afraid to tell anybody the things the Lord has done lest people think she isn't telling the truth or is senile!"

Only prayer-empowered work accomplishes true spiritual ends.

We must pray *before* we perform any service and *while* we are serving. Missionary Tom Daniel says, "Before I go witnessing, I claim the salvation of the lost people to whom we will talk, because Christ has already provided for their redemption on the cross. I ask him to take rightful possession of those he has already purchased."

"The Lord continues to teach me," states missionary Nelwyn Raborn, "that whatever I do in his name *must be bathed in prayer.* If otherwise, I fall flat on my face!"

Missionary Glenn Ingouf has been deeply impressed to pray before she does any kind of teaching by a statement in the book, *Power Through Prayer,* by E. M. Bounds. "Truth unquickened by God's Spirit deadens as much as, or more than, error." This made her aware how crucial prayer is to teaching.

Work can be a substitute for surrender, for faith, or for prayer.

In the same way, prayer can become a substitute for work, for surrender, or for faith.

Prayer *instead* of work becomes escapism. It is not meant to take the place of action.

The family's fox terrier, Pogo, had been terribly mangled in a fight. The veterinarian shook his head and told Roger Heidelberg, "He's partially paralyzed. If he lives, he'll be a long time recovering."

Since Pogo had been a member of the family for years, they dared ask the Lord that he might recover. "After all," wrote Heidelberg, "he who notices a sparrow might not mind helping a small dog."

For weeks Pogo's care involved changing his bed four or five times daily, massaging his muscles, suspending him in a sling, and forcing him to use his legs as he slowly recovered.

"Dog tired," Heidelberg collapsed in his easy chair late one evening after changing the dog's bed once again. "It surely would have been easier on us if you'd gone ahead and died," he said idly to the sleeping dog.

"I stiffened, shocked at my complaining that what we had prayed for was costing us more than I had counted on.

"What had I expected? That God would work a quick miracle, setting everything right again with only a token effort on my part? He could, of course. But why should he?

"Why should he provide cheap, convenient answers to our prayers? How dare we pray 'save the lost' unless we are witnessing to the lost ourselves? How dare we ask God for a better job unless we are giving our best to the job we now have? How dare we ask him to 'reach those in other countries' unless we are preparing to go or supporting those who are going?

"Pogo was used," he concluded, "to teach me something about prayer."[2]

"He who would work *must pray*."[3]

"He who would pray *must work*."[4]

Prayer instead of surrender is disobedience.

The person who prays for the lost world to know Jesus but is not willing to consider being a missionary is disobedient.

Rather than be hypocritical, many Christians just never pray for missions. They are afraid of what it might involve. They are like the young seminarian who had completed a masters degree and was working on a doctorate. In five years in seminary he had never attended a Missions Day in chapel, admitting he was afraid he might be called.

Prayer like all work requires energy, time, and concentration.

"Prayer is not for the lazy or the half-hearted," declares T. W. Hunt, "It is the hardest thing I do. I think prayer is work. It takes persistence and a tremendous act of the will.

"I am more easily distracted when I'm praying than any other time. Distractions nearly always prove Satan does not want us to pray. When I get distracted, I start praising the Lord and that brings me back to the point at hand."

Catherine Walker comments, "I react negatively when someone says 'prayer is work.'" That was a surprising statement to me from a person who is one of the hardest workers, accomplishes more and seems to enjoy it more than nearly anyone I know.

"It strikes me as something to dislike, want to avoid, and put off doing," she continued. "It does not make me want to pray. And I do not think that is what God wants it to be.

"Even in earnest prayer there should be a sense of relief that we can present our real and difficult problems to a wonderful God.

"Now if you say that prayer takes time, energy, and concentration I would agree with that. It certainly requires those. Even the word *effort* gives the wrong connotation in our society."

Determining whether or not prayer is work may depend on semantics or on our own personalities. But the authentic pray-er must realize the truth of Hunt's assertion:

"Prayer is the greatest challenge we have. We are frightened off by and at the same time drawn to a real challenge."

S. D. Gordon mentions five outlets of God's revealing his power through us:

"Through the life, what we are."

"Through the lips, what we say."

"Through our service, what we do."

"Through our money" [what we give].

"Through our prayer, what we claim in Jesus' name."

"And by all odds the greatest of these is the outlet through prayer."[5]

"Intercession is service: the chief service of a life on God's plan. It is superior in that it has fewer limitations."[6]

21
Prayer and Warfare

As Christians we are involved in spritual warfare on two fronts. We have an enemy without (Satan) and one within (self).

Anyone not counting on these two spiritual "givens" in the discipline of prayer is defeated before one starts. One will not understand why it is so hard to pray effectively or even to pray at all.

One of our Indonesian seminary students, Samosir of Sumatra, made a significant statement in a term paper he wrote on the doctrine of Satan: "In the West no one, not even Christians, believes in spirits because of scientific education. In the East everyone, including Christians, believes in spirits."

Christians may go to one of two extremes about Satan. As Samosir indicated, many Christians in recent decades have felt they have outgrown intellectually the doctrine of a personal devil, demon possession, and other such "medieval" holdovers. Others of this extreme may ignore the teaching, not considering it relevant to their Christian concept of love and light.

At the other extreme are Christians who are fearful or fascinated by a preoccupation with Satan and the forces of evil.

Whether Christians discarded the doctrine of Satan because of scientific education, religious pseudosophistication, religious psychology, or whatever, many have rediscovered its existence because the "world" revived it. Movies about demon possession, devil cults in the armed services and on college campuses, and occult practices among drug-culture adherents have challenged Christians to restudy the biblical teachings.

Know the enemy.

Satan is more powerful and more intelligent than any of us in the spiritual realm. He is the archenemy of God. He is not all-knowing, as is God, but he knows us better than we know ourselves.

God's word speaks of him always as our enemy and adversary and teaches that he is the god, prince, and ruler of the present world system. Entrusted with dominion of the earth by God, man succumbed to temptation and forfeited control to Satan by default.

Satan challenges God, thwarts his purposes, and seeks to nullify his word. Jesus called him the unclean spirit and the wicked or evil spirit, as well as the prince of demons. He labeled him the tempter, a murderer, a liar, and the father of lies.

He is the spirit now at work among the disobedient and is known as the destroyer and the accuser of believers.

Holding the power of darkness, Satan deceives the nations, blinds the minds of unbelievers, motivates evil among his followers, and seeks to devour and destroy persons.

He strives to lead us to gratify our physical nature, our pride, and personal desires. He pushes us to settle for the temporary, material, earthly values rather than for the eternal. He tempts by means of our natural human needs and desires, spiritual aspirations, and even Scripture.

The unseen ruler of this temporal world can transform himself into an angel of light and his agents into ministers of righteousness. He can counterfeit the works of God up to a point and produce counterfeit Christians.

Cunning and wise, he accuses us and causes us to doubt. He is allowed the power to attack us and cause us mental, emotional, and physical suffering.

The Living Bible's translation of satanic forces is enough to strike real fear in our hearts:

"For we are not fighting against people made of flesh and blood, but against persons without bodies—the evil rulers of this unseen world, those mighty satanic beings and great evil princes of darkness who rule this world; and against huge numbers of wicked spirits in the spirit world" (Eph. 6:12).

But Jesus says we are not to fear anyone except God, not even those who can kill us. God, he explained, is the only one who determines my eternal destiny (Luke 12:4-5). We are not to *fear* Satan. We are to *resist* him.

Withstanding the enemy.

We are not as strong or as wise as Satan. Stronger and wiser than he is, only God can stand against him. Jesus told us to *pray* to be delivered from evil. We cannot deliver ourselves. Therefore, our strength to resist Satan must come from God.

Peter warns us to be alert and cautious. "Be careful—watch out for attacks from Satan, your great enemy. He prowls around like a hungry, roaring lion, looking for some victim to tear apart" (1 Pet. 5:8, TLB). We are to expect his attacks and be alert to his strategy, knowing he will strike at either our weakest or strongest points, or both.

Battles have been won or lost on the watchfulness of the sentry. We must not be complacent, naive, or careless. We must not be foolishly self-sufficient.

This is the key to the very important counsel James gives us. "Submit yourselves therefore to God. Resist the devil, and he will flee from you" (Jas. 4:7). We are not to resist Satan in our own strength *before* we submit to God. If we do, we will fall. Entrusting ourselves to his protection and power comes first.

Jesus withstood Satan by recognizing temptations when they first entered his thoughts, by answering with Scripture and by bluntly telling Satan to leave him alone. He was able also to discern when Satan was using other persons like Peter to entice him.

We too need to recognize the enemy and withstand him in faith. God has promised us, "Every test that you have experienced is the kind that normally comes to people. But God keeps his promise, and he will not allow you to be tested beyond your power to remain firm; at the time you are put to the test, he will give you the strength to endure it, and so provide you with a way out" (1 Cor. 10:13, TEV).

Jesus is described as our advocate or defense attorney, defending us against the accusations and attacks of the prosecuting attorney, Satan, who accuses us day and night before the bar of God.

With the trials and tests God allows, Satan injects the temptations to doubt God, to turn against him and to lose our faith in his love and goodness. God allows Satan to test our faith as gold is tested and purified by fire, because our faith is far more precious to him than mere gold (1 Pet. 1:7, TLB).

Our warfare is also against the law of sin in our human nature, which wars against our souls. The present world system over which Satan rules is based on our human desires, our greedy ambitions, and the glamor of all we think splendid. It is opposed to God's real and permanent order. Satan seizes our evil desires to use as weapons of temptation when the tests come.

Overcoming the enemy.

We are fighting not only to defend ourselves against the devil's attacks but we are on the attack to liberate other persons and nations from his slavery.

"The truth is that, although we lead normal human lives, the battle we are fighting is on the spiritual level. The very weapons we use are not human but powerful in God's warfare for the destruction of the enemy's strongholds. Our battle is to break down every deceptive argument and every imposing defense that men erect against the true knowledge of God" (2 Cor. 10:3-5, Phillips).

The weapons of our warfare include faith, testimony, and prayer. We stand by faith in the death and finished work of Jesus our Savior on the cross. We overcome the accuser by the word of our testimony. And, according to Paul in Ephesians 6, when we are equipped with our armor we fight with prayer.

Christians have been likened to members of the underground resistance movement in Europe during World War II. Hitler had

98

driven out the Allied armies, taken over the governments on the Continent, and subjugated the peoples.

Freedom fighters were living in enemy territory, trying to thwart Hitler's forces and prepare for Allied liberation. At great risk to their lives, they communicated with Allied headquarters in London. The Nazis jammed their broadcasts, hunted down the transmitters, and tried relentlessly to keep messages from getting through. But the underground persevered, believing in ultimate victory and liberation by the Allies.

There are still enemies to be dealt with. But we can fight our battles in the knowledge that in Jesus' death and resurrection the decisive battle in God's war with Satan has been won. We can fight in confidence, staying in touch with our Command Post to guide us toward victory for us and for all of those who have been held captive by the enemies of God.

22
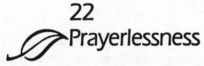Prayerlessness

Polls indicate most people believe in prayer. But the kind of prayer most non-Christians and probably a majority of Christians mean is not the kind taught in the Bible. Instead it is the fire-escape, self-centered, crisis-only kind.

Theoretically we believe in prayer. Actually we are practicing atheists when we run our lives as though God does not exist.

We *know* God exists, but many of us must admit we do not talk to him much, if at all, except for routine "blessings" at meals, superficial prayers in religious services, and when a crisis arises.

We do not pray because we really do not need anything. We are doing well enough on our own, thank you. We are even more foolish than the atheists. Or we are hypocrites, at best. We profess faith in God and many of us are committed to him as Lord and Master, the most important one in our life.

All we have to do to check our practice with our profession is calculate how much time we spend talking and listening to him, asking his advice, and waiting on his counsel. Most of us spend more time reading the newspaper or watching television, even if just the newscast.

A person does not have to intend to be a hypocrite to be one.

Nowhere are we more prayerless than in many of our churches and religious activities. We attend and conduct services, teach Bible classes, hold committee meetings, and perform many types of Christian work with little or no prayer. Prayerlessness is found from the pew to the pulpit.

Samuel Chadwick is quoted as saying, "The one concern of the devil is to keep Christians from praying. He fears nothing from prayerless studies, prayerless work, and prayerless religion. He laughs at our toil, mocks at our wisdom, but trembles when we pray."

Someone has diagnosed that "only the prayerless are too proud to admit to prayerlessness."

Tom Elliff, pastor of one of the nation's large and fast-growing churches until he resigned to become a missionary to Africa, began to study the lives of great people of prayer. He realized that persons dedicated to the practice of prayer were the ones God used to change history.

"The more I read the more convicted I became of my own prayerlessness. I had come, without benefit of human criticism or encouragement, under the searching eye of God. Alone before him I could not defend my utter lack of prayer."

Though he preached about prayer, conducted prayer meetings, and promised many people he would pray for them, he realized he just did not pray, except for spasmodic periods of renewed efforts. He decided on a "trial run," determining to spend the morning hours in uninterrupted prayer in his study. It seemed a difficult sacrifice for the busy pastor of a large urban church.

"When the office door closed behind me Monday morning, I

took my Bible, fell to my knees and told the Lord an out-and-out lie. 'Lord, you know how I have desired to have time alone with you in prayer.' In less time than it takes to tell it, the Lord reminded me that, for the most part, we do what we want to do. I was forced to agree that I had not had the time for prayer because I had not taken the time to pray."[1]

Honesty is the first piece of the Christian's armor. Elliff was open to the Spirit's convicting of sin and honest in his confession.

God hates lying, hypocrisy, pride—any barrier we try to erect between ourselves and him. One of the most dangerous things we do to ourselves is to deceive ourselves: to do something for one reason and convince ourselves it was for another.

We may say we do not pray because we are so busy, but God is the great discerner of motives and he wants us to be honest with ourselves.

Prayerlessness is sin. Ignoring God is rejecting him, and rejection is a form of hate. For Christians it is like saying to him, "I want your salvation and assurance of eternal life. I want your blessings and protection, but I don't want you."

Prayerlessness is saying to God, "I don't have time for you. I've got better and more important things to do." Or "You take care of your affairs, Lord, and I'll take care of mine. Don't call me. If I get in trouble, I'll call you." Or, "You tell me to pray, but I don't get much out of it. I can't see what it accomplishes. It's really more effort than I care to spend."

There are many reasons we do not pray. We do not feel the need, because we think we can do it ourselves. We are afraid to because it might cost too much in time, effort, and surrender. We do not think it would do any good because the situation is impossible. We nurse our secret doubts about the supernatural and disbelieve God. We intend to someday—but not yet.

Basically, we are prayerless because self, not God, is number one. The natural state of man is prayerlessness. Many of us, though Christians, are "carnal" or unspiritual Christians and our minds are consumed with human, temporal concerns.

"If there is one sin that hurts us more than all others," declares John Killinger, "it is surely the sin of not praying. We are meant to live in the Spirit of the Lord—to live joyously, vibrantly, and lovingly in the world. But if we do not pray we cannot live in the Spirit. It is as simple as that. We lack the 'daily connection' to God that would make such a wonderful life possible."[2]

Andrew Murray says prayerlessness is a reproach to God and the cause of deficient spiritual life. It is a dreadful loss for Christians whose pastors do not teach them to pray and makes taking the gospel to the world impossible.[3]

"Many feel that the great need of missions is the obtaining of men and women who will give themselves to the Lord to strive in prayer for the salvation of souls."[4]

Since prayer is meant to do God's work in the world, we miss the fulfillment of working with him to redeem his world and accomplish his worldwide purposes.

When her denomination began an emphasis on taking the gospel to every person in the world in this century, missionary Martha Franks was worried. "I did not hear much talk about prayer. And that idea will never get off the ground without prayer!" She likened it to a rocket sitting on the launching pad not going anywhere.

Prayer is the ignition to world evangelization. And every Christian can help launch it!

23
Prayer and Its Importance

Why do some missionaries say, "The most important thing you can do for us is pray"?

They seem to have learned with Andrew Murray that "in spiritual work, *everything depends on prayer*."[1]

If their statement seems an *over*statement to us, it may be we have not yet learned the absolute truth of or do not believe Jesus' declaration, "apart from me, you can do *nothing*" (John 15:5, RSV). Zero. Nothing.

Then how can it be that many of us have been in "religious" work for many years with little prayer and there seem to be results? Persons have been saved, churches have grown, and we seem to be succeeding.

I do not know. I can only guess. For one thing, God honors his Word. (Isa. 55:11). Second, not all of the results are truly spiritual ones (1 Cor. 3:12-15). For another, there probably have been unknown persons praying (Acts 10:22).

Also, as Jack Gray points out, in our churches "we never set personal goals we cannot reach. When we reach them, we, therefore, are successful. We have not learned our failures because we have never attempted what *we* ourselves cannot do."

The implication of his analysis is that we have not done very well in making disciples of all nations because we have not attempted what only God can do. We only do that in prayer!

"If God can do as much as he has with us with such elementary, perfunctory praying," Gray continues, "what *is* the potential?"

"You do not have because you do not ask" (Jas. 4:2, RSV), James says. And the Lord proclaims, "I was ready to answer my people's prayers but they did not pray. I was ready for them to find me, but they did not even try. The nation did not pray to me, even though I was always ready to answer, 'Here I am; I will help you'" (Isa. 65:1, TEV).

Prayer is a necessity for power in ministry.

"You can do *more* than pray," contends S. D. Gordon, "*after* you have prayed. But you can *not* do more than pray *until* you have prayed."

Many of us believe, he remarks, that we can serve and then pray to add power to our service. "*No,*" he exclaims. "We can do no thing of real power until we have [prayed]."[2]

In the preceding chapter we related how in Tom Elliff's search for a deeper prayer life, he decided to spend the mornings in uninterrupted prayer.

"I confess," continues Elliff, "that I frequently glanced at my watch during those first minutes of prayer. Each minute seemed to take forever. I discovered that I was really not accustomed to communion with God. I felt uncomfortable as I framed the words, thinking how they would sound to others. Praying for all the usual people, events, and needs did not dispel the uneasiness I felt. It was obvious God wanted to do business on a deeper level. He wanted to deal with my personal rebellion to his way. A greater barrier of unconfessed sin had to crumble under the forgiveness of God during the next few hours. Cleansed by the work of Jesus, according to 1 John 1:9, I could now see clearly the issues that confronted the members of my congregation. It was then I began to pray in earnest for them."

When he opened his door at noon that first day, Elliff found a stranger who had just been passing the church when "something" told him to go in and ask how he "could get saved." In a short while he was born into God's family and rushed home to lead his wife to accept Christ. Similar experiences occurred the next two days when he finished his prayer time. During the next two weeks, more than one hundred individuals responded to the invitations in Sunday services, over half of them professing faith in Christ as Savior.[3]

Called the "prince of preachers," Charles Haddon Spurgeon is quoted as saying, "I would rather teach one man to pray than ten men to preach." It is recorded that there was an audible hum in his church's auditorium as people prayed for him and the service.

Someone has said, "To arouse *one* man or woman to the tremendous power of prayer for others is worth more than the combined activity of a *score* of *average* Christians."

Watt expresses his conviction that "the greatest need of the church is to know how to pray."[4]

Prayer is a necessity for missions.

The Holy Spirit called the first two missionaries, Paul and Barnabas, during a prayer meeting. Other new thrusts and movements in world missions have been born of prayer.

"When we say that prayer is the very life-blood of mission," explains John V. Taylor, "we are not talking about one of several resources, like money and man-power and influence, which we muster to aid our enterprise; we are saying that the essential missionary activity is to live in prayer."[5]

Some contemporary Christians believe that the great missionary revival of the nineteenth century is due more to the prayer and consecration of David Brainerd than any other man. He was the sickly young man who felt such a burden for the American Indians. He could not speak their language and spent whole days alone in prayer praying to be filled with the Holy Spirit so they could comprehend his message. He knew he was completely dependent on the Holy Spirit's power to interpret to them and prayed until revival swept them.

As he was dying of consumption in Jonathan Edwards' home, Brainerd's prayers so inspired his host that Edwards wrote the great appeal for Christendom to unite in prayer for the conversion of the world. His life story touched William Carey, Henry Martyn, Robert Murray McCheyne, and others who became missionaries.

"True intercession in the service of the Christian mission is the purest acknowledgment that the mission is God's, not ours."[6]

Prayer is a personal necessity.
"Prayer is one of the basic priorities of life, like eating, sleeping, working, and going to church," claims missionary Indy Whitten.

"My own concept developed over the years," says missionary Barbara Vick, "is that prayer is my spiritual lifeline—my spiritual 'umbilical cord.' Without it I am helpless and in danger of dying."

Prayer is the most important service.
"The greatest thing any one can do for God and man is to pray," S. D. Gordon was convinced. "It is not the only thing. But it is the chief thing.

"The great people of earth to-day are the people who pray. I do not mean those who talk about prayer; nor those who say they believe in prayer; nor yet those who can explain about prayer; but I mean those who *take* time and *pray*.

"They have not time. It must be taken from something else. This something else is important. Very important, and pressing, but still less important and less pressing than prayer. [These] are people who put prayer first and group the other items in life's schedule around and after prayer.

"These are the people to-day who are doing the most for God; in winning souls; in solving problems; in awakening churches; in supplying both men and money for mission posts; in keeping fresh and strong [those] lives far off in sacrificial service on the foreign field where the thickest fighting is going on; in keeping the old earth sweet awhile longer.

"It is wholly a secret service. . . .

"God will do as a result of the praying of the humblest one here what otherwise he *would* not do. Yes, I can make it stronger than that, and I must make it stronger, for the Book does. Listen: God will do in answer to the prayer of the weakest one here what otherwise He *could* not do"[7]

24
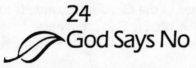God Says No

Like a loving parent, God often says no when we ask. Like children, we may not understand why. We do not like no. We much prefer yes.

At some point in our praying, if we are submitted and sensitive to him, God often impresses us that the answer is no. Moses, Jeremiah, Paul, and Jesus all experienced and recognized his saying *no*.

Moses was refused entrance into the Promised Land (Deut. 3:23-28). Because he had disobeyed before the whole nation, they must see how seriously God regards disobedience. God rejected Jeremiah's plea that Israel be spared punishment (Jer. 7:16). It was too late.

Paul appealed for God to remove "a thorn in the flesh," possibly, a painful or humiliating physical ailment (2 Cor. 12:7-10). Perhaps strong-willed Paul required a reminder of his absolute dependence on the Lord, as well as needing to experience and exemplify how great is his enabling strength when we are helpless.

Jesus asked God to provide another way of saving mankind, if it were possible at all (Matt. 26:39,42). When he sensed this was not what his Father willed, his praying changed. "Since there does not seem to be any other way," he seems to express it, "I surrender and want what you want for me."

He had not felt well all fall, but Tom Law attributed it to an overload of work and thought it might be a recurring ulcer. He and Betty had served eight years in Cuba under the Home Mission Board and were now in their seventeenth year in Spain where, under the Foreign Mission Board, he had served as mission treasurer, as well as field missionary, pastor, book deposit manager, promoter of literature ministry, visiting seminary professor, and several times mission chairman.

Though he planned a checkup in the United States during a February trip on mission business, his increasing discomfort took him to a doctor in mid-January. X-rays were made and the Spanish doctor made an immediate diagnosis: cancer of the colon. Surgery was needed immediately since the colon was almost closed.

A series of "small" miracles enabled Tom to board a flight the next day to Houston, his hometown, and four days later he was in surgery. Betty concluded his treasurer's business and followed.

The doctors informed her there was little hope. The cancer had spread to the pancreas, the lymph system, abdominal wall, and liver. When he learned the truth, Tom indicated he would face it with determination as he had faced every other challenge in life.

During postoperative care, he remarked that he had preached much about faith during the years of his ministry and now he was to have the opportunity to live it. With the doctor's poor prognosis, he knew his recovery would depend on a miracle if the Lord so willed. "We asked for a miracle of complete healing," said Betty. "During the weeks he was battling the malignancy and also the side effects of the medication, we did not talk about death. We knew the odds against us. The doctors had indicated from two months to two years. We felt it would be poor faith to admit the possiblity of death if we were praying for a miracle of healing.

"Tom felt his life had been spared many times in the past and knew if God still had work for him to do, we would see our miracle."

Two months later jaundice brought new tests and scans and talk of more drastic treatment. "That afternoon we talked much about the possibility of death," Betty continued, "because we knew they were grasping at straws with the proposed treatment." The morning after new treatment was administered, the doctor told Betty that Tom could not live because of the liver's rapid deterioration.

"God did have a further work for Tom," declared Betty. "It was to teach us how to die." During the final eight days of his life when he knew he was dying, Tom actively taught the members of his family, friends, and medical staff that the one who trusts Christ has no reason to fear. He showed that dying is a part of living and death is an entering into a new phase of eternal life.

"The last eight days were unique. Our son, Tom III, returned from Paraguay where he is a missionary, only five days before his dad's death. In the last days of his earthly life Tom was surrounded by his four sons, something so very special since our family had been separated so much these last years.

"We had a family worship service in which Tom participated. Afterwards there was a time of saying good-bye as we prepared to see him off on another 'trip,' knowing that one day we would be reunited with no more separation. In an uncanny way what he said came only from God, he knew what each of us needed. His text for those days was Philippians 1:21: 'For to me to live is Christ, and to die is gain.'

"Tom's slogan in life was 'Let's press on.' He worked until the day he left Spain and this is the way he liked it. As active as he was, we are grateful he did not have the frustration or suffering of a long illness.

"Many persons wrote saying they were praying for us . . . for strength, for healing, etc. One well-meaning friend wrote, quoting Scripture to buttress her opinion that, if we had faith, Tom would be healed. There seemed to be no allowance for God's will. In effect, the amount of faith we had would determine whether God answered affirmatively. We did not find her letter helpful or encouraging.

"We believed God could heal. But he did not. Even as Christians, we often fear death and the unknown, but God has taken away any fear I had.

"God gave us many special answers to prayer, including the gift of thanksgiving which caused us to see his countless blessings when it would have been easier to feel defeated; friends ministered to us; our first family reunion in eighteen months; and many 'little miracles.'

"We did not receive the 'big miracle' we asked for: Tom's physical healing. In Spain it is customary to say 'What God wills. . . .' I do not believe God caused Tom's cancer. He created a world of natural order. Scientists indicate that cancer occurs when something goes wrong with the natural order. I believe God can perform miracles and reestablish the natural order of things, if it is his will. We prayed for a miracle. We do not know why we did not receive it.

"But we believe God knows the future and what is best for his children. Within the circumstances we brought to him, God has showered us with blessings, peace, and comfort. The many blessings of Tom's illness, especially the last eight days, added up to a 'big miracle,'" Betty concluded.

I listened to an interview about faith and healing with a nationally known religious personality to whom God had evidently given the gift of healing. "I have never said that I have healed anyone," she insisted. "Only God can heal.

"And I have never said that if a person has enough faith, he will be healed. That would be very cruel. I have seen persons with great faith who were not healed. Others who came as spectators or who did not expect to be healed were healed.

"Why God heals some and not others," she pondered, "I do not know. That is in the sovereignty of God alone. Only he knows."

The sovereignty of God also means he does not have to explain his decisions. His only answer to Job's desperate questions about his suffering was the answer that he is God. But that was enough for Job. It is enough for me. It is enough for Betty Law.

I feel sure as we sit at his feet around the heavenly throne he will explain why there were times he had to say no to our deepest longings and prayers.

This life is not the summit of our existence. God is. This life is merely the scaffolding on which we prepare for the next. The fetus in a womb is preparing for life in this world. Those of us in this life are getting ready for the next. Our ultimate home is God. Forever.

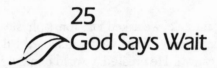

25
God Says Wait

"God has answered, not exactly in the way we all prayed," report missionaries Jay and Laura Lee Stewart, "but he has provided what is needed."

Needed was a larger, better press for the Eastern Africa publications ministry and a new folding machine to replace a twenty-six-year-old one for which spare parts were no longer available.

For several years interested pray-ers in America had joined missionaries and nationals in praying for the equipment. For three years the request had been approved by the publication board, the local mission organization, and the Foreign Mission Board for allocation from the annual foreign missions offering.

But overwhelming worldwide needs for funds and high inflation rates meant that gifts did not reach far enough.

Used presses are seldom available in their area, explain the Stewarts, and, if sold, are rarely in good shape. Yet a local printer wanted to sell one that was clean, well-maintained, in excellent condition, and less than four years old. The oldest small offset press was taken in trade. A new press would have cost $85,000, but the entire package cost $27,000.

"We had prayed for a new press and folder," they said. "You have been faithful to pray. God answered, not with $125,000, but with a combination of circumstances and resources to provide what was needed."

Why did God delay? Why did he not provide *new* equipment? Was it to save money? Or to involve intercessors in his work? Or to accent the financial needs of the foreign mission enterprise? Was it to give a witness to the African printer? Was it to develop faith and endurance in the publications staff?

Only the Lord knows *all* the reasons our prayers are not answered when and how we ask, though some reasons are obvious from Scripture and personal observation.

Common sense tells us it would not be good for us if God always gave *what* we ask *when* we ask. According to Russell H. Dilday, Jr., Christians have experienced enough answers to prayer to know it works and enough failures to realize it is not magic.

Daniel's experience teaches us that Satan can block or delay God's answer (Dan. 10:12-13). James also tells us that we do not receive answers to our prayers when we ask "amiss" (Jas. 4:3), that is, with wrong motives to use for our own selfish desires.

God waits for us to learn some truth, change some attitude, confess some sin, obey some command, or surrender some disobedience that blocks his will for us or others.

Since a small child Ann had prayed for her father, but her prayers were not answered. She had not felt close to him because he was not the Christian father she longed for, and was not an easy person to know. His treatment of her mother caused resentment.

Active in church in her teen years, she shared her problem with a pastor who reminded her of the verse, "If any one says, 'I love God,' and hates his brother, he is a liar" (1 John 4:20, RSV). "I felt no one could understand," she lamented. "I *did* love God, but I *couldn't* love Daddy."

Some years later as a pastor's wife on a short-term English-language assignment overseas, she attended a Baptist Woman's meeting. "James 4:3 about praying 'amiss' jumped out at me," she recalled.

"As I thought about my prayers for my father, I realized for the first time I had never really prayed for him. I had used the words, 'Save Daddy,' 'Make Daddy go to church,' 'Change Daddy,' and without verbalizing it, was also saying, 'so our family will be happier,' 'so my mother's life will be happier,' 'so that I will have the kind of father I want.'

"I was not praying for Daddy. I was praying for myself and Mother. Confessing this to God, I saw I had been a stumbling block to Daddy because of my attitude. I began to see him differently, as someone God loves, just the way he is. For the first time in my life I could pray 'I love Daddy. I want him to be saved. I want him to have a saving relationship with you, Lord, but I love him now just the way he is.'

"After twenty-five years I was finally truly praying for Daddy." For three years after returning to the United States Ann learned to love her dad more each time she prayed for him and was around him. There were opportunities to witness to him.

A new struggle was introduced when her husband felt a strong call to career overseas missions. "How can I go half-way around the world to tell people about Jesus when I cannot reach Daddy?" she argued with the Lord. "He's in poor health. He could die any time. How can I leave him with no certainty that I will ever see him again?"

Eventually came surrender and the assurance of knowing she was doing God's will and later there was peace in prayer as she felt God would take care of her father. Not long afterwards her mother shared news of her father's confession of faith. Visits with them before leaving for the mission field confirmed the change in her parents' homelife and the father's transformation from a hard and bitter person.

"I am thankful the Lord allowed me to see that miracle come to pass," she said, "but I'm also thankful for the miracle in my own life when God opened my eyes to my selfish, immature prayer life. Our love for a person cannot depend on God's changing them. It must come first."

Adapting the saying, "Prayer changes things," missionaries Fred

112

and Linda Beck declare, "prayer enables God to change us to meet new situations."

Missionary Charles Hampton would agree. "In twenty-four years of asking the Lord to open the door to missions or remove my call, he neither removed the circumstances that blocked our going nor the sharpness of the call. In those years I learned to wait as he taught and trained me in the school of 'hard knocks.'"

Eventually God led the Hamptons to a country with long-standing Christian work, well-established churches, mature pastors, and conditions to challenge all their abilities. He realizes now the preparation was necessary.

God not only delays answering prayer to prepare for more effective, wide-reaching service, but he takes the long look. He wants the best for us in relation to his Kingdom's work over the years.

On their fourth assignment in Africa, Sam and Ginny Cannata began work in a new country among a people who had little gospel witness. With only six weeks of language tutoring by a Wycliffe missionary, they were left with little way to communicate the Christian faith other than Sam's medical work and Ginny's literacy classes.

Prayer partners in the United States were asked to pray that the only available young man would be willing to leave Bible school in another country where he was studying and return to his native area to teach the Cannatas and preach to his people. He did not accept the invitation.

The Wycliffe missionaries returned the following year and again the young man, Idris Kieda, was invited to return and help with the Bible's translation. Still he was not interested but promised to pray.

As he prayed he remembered a recurring dream he had experienced weeks before. Three times one night he had dreamed he was preaching back home in a small, new church. As he preached there and in other places in the area many people responded to accept Jesus. At the time he had not understood the dream. When it was recalled as he prayed, he felt the Lord was directing him to return.

"God's timing was not our timing," Ginny emphasizes. "It was better. If he had returned when *we* asked him, we know now we would have depended on him and would not have learned the language as well as we did.

"But we had prayed, our prayers remained before the throne,[2] and at the right time God released his power in Idris's life."

Delayed answers to prayer can deepen our personal relationship to the Lord, deepen our compassion for others with problems, and result in praise to God's glory.

"My greatest experience of answered prayer took fifteen years," exclaims missionary Mildred Cagle. "In the process my son went from rebellious teenager to complete rebellion against God and all the principles he had been taught and back again to God.

"Viewing the whole experience now, I praise the Lord for what my son is today. God protected and wooed him back. His sustaining grace to me was like a miracle."

In the process of our waiting for God to answer our prayers, he produces in us endurance, faith, and mature character. Often ordinary pray-ers are developed into steadfast intercessors.

When God says wait, it is because he has a better vantage point. He can see the whole and he takes the long look. He knows spiritual and eternal values are best. He wants us to believe that, too.

26
Prayer and Persistence

We have two choices as a Christian. We can pray. Or we can get discouraged, give up, and quit.

"Men ought always to pray, and not to faint" (Luke 18:1), is the most familiar translation of what Jesus desired for his followers. "To faint" also means to "lose heart." I have trouble persisting when the result does not come fairly soon after I have prayed, especially if I have prayed sincerely several times.

But *The Living Bible* paraphrases it best, I think: "Jesus told his disciples a story to illustrate their need for constant prayer and to show them that they must keep praying until the answer comes."

Jesus told the two parables that puzzle many, about the reluctant friend (Luke 11:5-13) and the unjust judge (Luke 18:1-8), to encourage us to pray with confidence. Dr. Ray Summers explains, "The central teaching is not that man can, by repeated prayer, break down the will of God. It is rather that man can be encouraged in prayer by the realization that he prays to a just God who desires to give and to do that which his child needs.

"If a man can get from a friend what he does not desire to give, and if a woman can get an unjust judge to do what he does not want to do, how much more can one be encouraged that he will receive from a God who delights to give. Because he is a just God, he will do the right thing without being begged."[1]

In the parable of the man who persisted in begging bread from his neighbor for his visiting friends, the *New English Bible* states, "The very shamelessness of the request will make him get up and give him all he needs" (Luke 11:8). R. A. Torrey believes God wants us to draw near to him so determined to obtain the things we seek that we will not be shamed "by any seeming refusal or delay on God's part. God delights in the holy boldness that will not take 'no' for an answer. It is an expression of great faith and nothing pleases God more than faith."[2]

God knows it takes time to perfect our faith and obedience in prayer. He wants us to be complete and mature. The process of establishing in us a strong, unshakable confidence in him takes time. If it were quick and easy, we would not develop strength of Christian character.

It would be out of step with the rest of life if we could pray for something and always get it the first or second time we asked. Many of the best things in life require years of hard work and real effort.

We do not fully appreciate achievements gained easily or things

115

acquired quickly. No newly marrieds buying a whole household of furniture could ever appreciate it as much as a couple who labors, scrapes, and saves for each purchase.

A couple praying for a son or daughter who strays momentarily but returns quickly may be deeply grateful. But it is doubtful they can know the depth of gratitude, joy, and ecstatic praise to the Lord experienced by parents who have prayed months and even years for a wayward child who eventually returns to the ways of the Lord.

I do not mean that praying is a work of achievement. Rather God would train us by the process of endurance. "There is no more blessed training in prayer," declares R. A. Torrey, "than that which comes through being compelled to ask again and again and again even through a long period of years before one obtains that which he seeks from God."[3]

Martin R. Smith of Dynapac advises business executives to reward and encourage perseverance above all other virtues. "Managers with raw determination, a willingness to press on even during the darkest hours, should be hired quickly and cultivated with enthusiasm," he counsels, "because they can move mountains for the company."[4]

He quotes a statement by Calvin Coolidge framed on the walls of many successful companies that says it all:

PRESS ON

Nothing in the world can take the place of perseverance.
Talent will not; nothing is more common than unsuccessful
    men with talent.
Genius will not; unrewarded genius is almost a proverb.
Education will not; the world is full of educated derelicts.
Perseverance and determination alone are omnipotent.[5]

Most of us can remember persons we have known who were not the most talented or gifted but who had determination to succeed. There are athletes, musicians, artists, businessmen, scholars, preachers, and politicians, who had less innate ability, talent, skill, or education than many they have surpassed in achievement, simply because they kept practicing and working toward their goal.

116

Someone close to the family of an internationally ranked male tennis star revealed that he and his brother had started taking lessons and playing together while still very young. The brother actually had more innate ability but lacked the determination to practice and to win each game. Finally, at one point, the family decided to concentrate everything on the persistent son. He made up for ability by tenacity and rose to the top.

There are times when we pray for something one time and have the impression that we have done all we should or can. To pray for it a second time indicates lack of faith. But there are other times when we need to make the same request many times.

"We should be careful about what we ask from God," warns Torrey, "but when we do begin to pray for a thing we should never give up praying for it until we get it, or until God makes it very clear and very definite to us that it is not His will to give it."[6]

To quit before that point, he says, means we are spiritually lazy, not that it is not God's will.

Just as in anything else, the difference between success and failure in prayer could be praying one more time.

Dottie Hayes quotes a praying aunt she has heard say many times, "Don't ask me to pray about anything unless you really mean it. I'll pray until the answer comes."

27
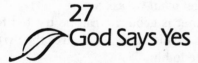God Says Yes

Prayer is meant for answers. It is not primarily to achieve or receive, but to be with God. If, however, we do not observe some results, prayer will lose its meaning for most Christians.

Many say prayer is mainly for what it does to us. It changes our attitudes and viewpoints. And that may be so. Only mature Christians seem to keep on keeping on when nothing happens. But if that is *all*, most of us will quit.

When we do not get answers, we stop asking. Unfortunately this

117

may be what has happened to so many believers. We did not get what we prayed for. Our prayers "failed," or so we thought. So many of us have given up praying except for ritual or in crises.

Most Christians have not been taught that

- Praying is absolutely necessary to vital Christian living.
- Prayer is a continuous learning process.
- There are definite reasons our praying fails.
- God wants us to learn how to pray.

If Jesus had instructed his disciples only once that we are to pray, that would be enough. But he tells us many times. He says it backward and forward and in many ways. Perhaps so we would not miss it, Jesus told us three times in one statement that we should pray. The tense is continuous:

"Keep on asking and the gift will be given you; keep on seeking and you will find; keep on knocking and the door will open to you" (Matt. 7:7, Williams).[1]

Then he underlined it and nailed it down:

"For everyone who keeps on asking, receives, and everyone who keeps on seeking, finds, and to the one who keeps on knocking, the door will open" (Matt. 7:8, Williams).

Six times in two sentences he tells us to pray. How much plainer can he make it? He *means* for us to pray. And he promises results!

Until recently I had not noticed an interesting detail: Jesus does not promise we will necessarily get *what* we ask for.

The key follows: since the Father is good, he can be trusted to give us the very best gifts. As the saying goes, "God gives the *very best* to those who leave the choice to him."

Luke says God will give us the very best gift of all if we ask: the Holy Spirit (Luke 11:13). He ensures that we get all we need and much more besides. "To receive God's Holy Spirit is to receive the totality of God's gifts," according to Ray Summers.[2]

This also tells us we cannot manipulate God. He comes *with* his gifts. Carnal man would bypass him to have what he gives.

Because we are selfish and self-centered, we feel that everything in the world has been provided just for us. "We think and act as

118

though everything, inanimate things, plants, animals, human beings, even our own souls, were created for the purpose of bringing gratification to our selfish desires.

"And we make no exception of God.

"As soon as we encounter Him, we immediately look upon Him as another means of getting our own ends. . . .

"The natural man looks upon prayer, too, in this light. . . . This is the reason why the natural man seldom finds it pays to pray regularly to God. It requires too much effort, takes too much time and is on the whole impracticable."[3]

If you have tried praying and not had much success, if you know you should pray but do not feel like it, if you want to pray but do not know how, if you are just not able—in fact, you have given up— that is great! You are just coming to the place God can help you. Listen:

"Prayer and helplessness are inseparable. . . . Your helplessness is your best prayer. . . . Do not be anxious because of your helplessness. Above all, do not let it prevent you from praying. Helplessness is the real secret and impelling power of prayer. You should therefore rather try to thank God for the feeling of helplessness which he has given you. It is one of the greatest gifts God can impart to us. . . .

"Prayer therefore consists simply in telling God day by day in what ways we feel we are helpless."[4]

God tells us to pray simply, sincerely, and directly. We insult him by rattling off meaningless, set or memorized phrases. We cannot fool or impress him. We just *tell* him in our own way. God is Person. He is a Father who knows us better than we know ourselves and still loves us.

Catherine Walker reminds us that "Paul taught, 'Let your requests be made known unto God [Phil. 4:6].' Jesus said, 'Ask and ye shall receive.' Have we no requests and strong desires to express to God?

"It is better to ask and get a *no* than not to ask. Asking is our business. Answering is God's business. We do not need to protect God's reputation by not challenging him with our asking. God, as God, can manage the results of our praying. We are the ones who fail by not asking.

"In teaching people to thank God and not always be praying 'Gimme, gimme, gimme,' we have experienced overkill. Adults ask for almost nothing.

"Even in the beautiful prayers of Christian leaders I sense a strong reluctance to ask God for anything. The prayers tell God *about* problems, situations, and coming events. Names of family, friends, even missionaries are mentioned.

"But almost nothing is requested. Let's pray bold 'gimme' prayers for a lost world and for God's kingdom to come."

Once we have learned to come simply with our own personal needs to the Father, then we can begin to pray with confidence for others.

"The Father gives the Holy Spirit to them that ask Him, not least, but most, when they ask for others."[5]

William E. Davidson, ninety-one, seasoned intercessor, feels he is stronger physically now than at fifty. He jogs a mile and exercises twenty minutes each morning.

During the day, he prays for approximately 450 missionaries by name, using cards on which he has written items of need or special petitions by their name and place of service. He has corresponded with most of them until it became too expensive.

When Davidson returned from missionary service in Chile in 1923 because of acute miliary tuberculosis, the doctors gave him three months to live. In those days there were no drugs for treatment.

Both Chilean and U.S. Christians prayed for him. He surprised doctors by recovering to the point of being allowed to serve again in Chile. However, recurrence of the T.B., this time cervical, caused his resignation and permanent return to the States. Over a period of twenty years he was finally clear of active T.B. and complications and had gained normal strength again.

"It takes me about three hours to pray for all the missionaries. I don't do it all at one time. About every six months I have to recopy my cards as I handle them so much."

He began his prayer ministry by praying for the individual Chile missionaries and Chilean Christians, then gradually added names of persons he read about or met at conferences and conventions. When the number reached 450, he tapered off, feeling that was the limit of what he could handle.

Davidson is especially sensitive to pray for missionaries experiencing chronic or debilitating illnesses, accidents, crisis, or situations requiring leaves of absence. He recounts many victories of healing, restoration, and return to fields of service.

A typical entry would include a couple in a war-torn country, the wife, a former student when he served as college professor of religion. "With others I have been praying they would not be hit by flying shells or their hospital damaged. They have been protected, and though their hospital was a bit damaged sometime ago, it has been repaired."

A small child learns to work by following a parent around and imitating what the parent does. Paul uses this picture in telling us to "Follow God's example in everything you do just as a much loved child imitates his father" (Eph. 5:1, TLB).

Jesus' work is intercession. "He is able to save forever those who draw near to God through Him, since He always lives to make intercession for them" (Heb. 7:25, NASB). Therefore, we want to learn to do what he does.

"Intercession is the climax of prayer."[6]

28
Prayer and Pocketbooks

What do our pocketbooks have to do with our prayer life?
Everything!
That's what Jesus said!
"You cannot serve both God and money" (Luke 16:13, TEV).

Wonder why the King James translators of the Bible translated mamōnā as "mammon"? Was it as touchy a subject then as today? Were they as materialistic as we? Did the statement step on their toes as much as on ours? Did they try to ignore it as we do?

"When the Pharisees heard all this, they made fun of Jesus because they loved money" (Luke 16:14, TEV). Blunt talk like that is not popular. I have heard pastors and church members criticize certain plain-talking missionaries who pointed out how little we give to missions as compared to what we spend on ourselves and our churches. They did not want them in their churches again because they were "too negative."

Jesus spoke more about materialism than about prayer.

He said something else just as startling to those of us who would aspire to become pray-ers. "Whoever is faithful in small matters will be faithful in large ones; whoever is dishonest in small matters will be dishonest in large ones. If, then, you have not been faithful in handling worldly wealth, how can you be trusted with true wealth?" (Luke 16:10-11, TEV).

The implication seems to be, "If you are not using your material means to further God's kingdom, how can God trust you with spiritual power in prayer?"

Earlier Jesus had warned, "Watch out and guard yourselves from every kind of greed [covetousness]; because a person's true life is not made up of the things he owns, no matter how rich he may be" (Luke 12:15, TEV). Paul cautions that "no immoral or impure person or covetous man, who is an idolater, has an inheritance in the kingdom of Christ and God" (Eph. 5:5, NASB). Being covetous or greedy is the same as being an idol worshiper. We put "things" in the place of God. It is also classed with immorality.

How can we tell if we are covetous? Ask yourself two questions:

When will I have enough? Most of us feel it is in the future; when we get "just a little bit more."

Do I have a shopping list of "wants"? Most of us have a mental record of things we plan to buy when we get the money. We are not yet satisfied. Bluntly speaking, we are covetous.

The Tenth Commandment commands us not to covet our

neighbor's house, spouse, servant, ox, ass, "nor any thing that is thy neighbor's" (Ex. 20:17).

Technically, it may have meant not to crave what belongs to one's neighbor, but the fuller meaning is not even to yearn for something *like* our neighbor's. In other words, desiring to "keep up with the Joneses" is wrong.

"*Idolatry* is an ugly word to Christians," declares Cecil Ray, executive director of North Carolina Baptists. "Less ugly but still not attractive is the term 'secularism.' However, the term 'the good life' is pleasing to many Christians. The fact that in America all three mean the same is seldom understood or even considered.

"Let one fact be clear: there is not enough money for Christians to properly support the worldwide missions task of our Lord and at the same time support a personal lifestyle shaped by American good life standards.

"There can be no great advance in . . . missions," Ray emphasizes, "apart from an equally great commitment by members and churches in lifestyle."[1]

Are our churches being "faithful in small matters" when the missionaries in Harare (Salisbury), Zimbabwe, have a monthly budget of seventy dollars to evangelize a city of 568,000 persons, while many Sunday School groups spend more than that in one night on a class dinner?

The Malawi Baptist mission absorbed three new missionary families one year recently with only a 5 percent budget increase, doing it gladly because they so needed and wanted new missionaries. "We watched," wrote Rebecca Phifer, "as each missionary voluntarily cut his budget in order to give critically needed items to the others." Assigned a new vehicle, one man noted a new missionary would be driving in some especially rugged areas. "I don't need the new car as badly as he will," he insisted. "I want him to have it."

American Christians have made two assumptions about our prosperity, according to Ray. "First, we assume it is proper for 'the privileged people' [such as in the United States] to have more than enough regardless of what happens to other people; and, second, the reward for being a faithful Christian is increased prosperity."[2]

The hunger and poverty of our world demand that we reassess our life-styles as Christians. Indulging in luxury and extravagance in our homes and churches while missionaries lack money to evangelize the world surely fits what Jesus said about being unfaithful with our material means.

What do our pocketbooks have to do with prayer? "If you refuse to listen to the cry of the poor," warns the writer of Proverbs, "your own cry for help will not be heard" (Prov. 21:13, TEV).

"There is perhaps no greater hindrance to prayer than stinginess, the lack of liberality toward the poor and toward God's work,"[3] declares R. A. Torrey.

George Mueller, known for his power in praying, handled over one million pounds sterling in the Lord's work. He was a "mighty man in prayer because he was a mighty giver," says Torrey. "What he received from God never stuck to his fingers; he immediately passed it on to others. He was constantly receiving because he was constantly giving."[4]

Missionary Yvonne Helton tells how the Lord spoke to her about life-style and led her to dedicate her material possessions to him. "I'd always thought that the churches were to send and I was to spend. I've always tithed. I've always given a lot. I said, 'Lord, I'm a single missionary. I've given my life. I've left my family and comforts of American life. And now, you want me to give more?'

"I went through my house, room to room, and said, 'Lord, it's all yours.' I came to my piano and the Lord said, 'That's what I want.' 'That, Lord? Take anything else!' I argued. 'It gives me great pleasure. It's the only possession I really owned when I was appointed.'

"He led me to give it to the church. It now serves as a symbol of his constant provision, love, and care and as a reminder of his total control of my life. Seventeen persons studied piano in our church last year."

The challenge of voluntary reduction grows clearer and louder. As author Ron Sider says, "We're not called to simple life-style because poverty is good. We are committed to Jesus Christ and to being faithful participants in his mission to a lost, broken world. It

124

is because two-and-a-half billion people have never heard the gospel and because one billion are malnourished, that Western Christians must drastically simplify their life-styles."[5]

Torrey points out what a pittance the orthodox churches of this country contribute on the average per year per member to missions. "When one thinks of the selfishness of the professing church to-day . . . it is no wonder the church has so little power in prayer. If we would get from God, we must give to others,"[6]

29
Prayer and Laborers

"If you saw ten men carrying a log, nine men on one end and one man on the other, which end would you help carry?"

God used that question in calling Borden of Yale, the young millionaire, to the mission field. Setting out for China, he never got beyond Egypt where he died of spinal meningitis. But his life has inspired thousands to Christian living and his question has called others to the fields of the world.

That searching question and a strong statement were among many factors God used to call me to the mission field. The one from a book and the other from a professor. Both related to unequal statistics.

Exposing the disproportion of money and men to win 5 percent of the world's population in the United States, Dr. J. W. MacGorman in New Testament class decried the disparity that only three and one-half cents of every Southern Baptist dollar and only one out of every 123 preachers went overseas to witness to approximately 95 percent of the world: "I say it reverently, but I say it firmly: God is not that stupid a general! He cannot be blamed for this strategy!"

In the thirty years since I heard Dr. MacGorman's strong statement, the Southern Baptist Convention has doubled in membership, but the proportion has not improved much if at all. Five percent of the seminaries' graduates go overseas to witness to 95 percent of the world.

It takes nearly five thousand Southern Baptists to field one career missionary. There are around 30,000 active ministers in our Convention not including countless ones now engaged in other fields and jobs, while there are 477 ordained ministers working in church evangelism overseas.

William R. Wakefield, the Foreign Mission Board's director of South and Southeast Asia, reports 415 missionaries for one billion people in his area or one missionary for every 2.5 million persons. There are 85 designated evangelists or church planters, which means one for every 12.5 million people. That is equivalent to about one pastor for the whole Southern Baptist Convention and 18 for the entire United States of America.

Has God's strategy not improved? I also ask reverently, but seriously.

Why should you and I have the gospel when millions do not? Is it that God loves us more? Or is it that someone told us of his love?

If we ask, "Are persons really lost without Jesus Christ as Savior?" we are asking the wrong question. The proper question is, "Are we really saved if we do not tell them of his love?" The early Christians couldn't help but tell what God had done for them.

Nowhere can we be more directly and strategically involved in missions than to pray as Jesus commanded us for the Lord of the harvest to thrust out laborers into his harvest (Luke 10:2).

Debbie Malone felt overwhelmed in her role as wife of the church's minister of music, mother of three children, and schoolteacher, along with several duties at church. She asked a month's leave of absence from leading the girls' missionary organization while she and her husband took on the added stress of seeking God's will about their place of service overseas. They attended a missionary candidates' conference and felt impressed toward a South American nation.

In her absence, Debbie's co-worker had led the girls to study the steps in becoming a missionary. Their mission magazine had presented prayer requests, which included one for music missionaries in a South American country. The girls had been especially interested in and prayed for that request. They did not know their minister of music and his wife were seeking God's will about missions.

When Debbie and Bob returned and shared their decision with the church family, the girls were thrilled to see how God works. "And it was wonderful for us to experience such dynamic response through intercessory prayer.

"I had always thought," said Debbie, "that somewhere there was somebody whose praying had helped me find God's design for my life. But never had a 'someone' shared with me that that person was part of God's answered prayer in my life."

Missionaries Wally and Betty Poor introduce with great pride the young man who pastors the church the Poors started years earlier in a warehouse. They feel the Lord chose him and began grooming him from the day of his conversion to replace Wally as pastor. He was won to the Lord long before the Poors met him, in another city on April 8, 1972, when American Christians were praying for Wally on his birthday.

"We have sinned against the harvest of souls by failing to pray the Lord for laborers; and it is evident that prayerlessness has produced a great lack of workers. This is sin against men over the world." These words were penned by "Preacher" Hallock, whose own son, E. F. Hallock Jr., is a career missionary.[1]

"There are people on the foreign mission fields who should never have been there," believes O. Hallesby. "At the same time there are people here at home who should have been missionaries.

"This is our own fault. We should have prayed about this important matter, prayed that none might be sent out who were not sent of God; and at the same time that those whom God has chosen might not remain at home but really go out into foreign lands."[2]

As we pray, we must not close our hearts against the possibility God may call us. Praying ones are the persons sensitive enough to hear his voice.

It happened as Isaiah was praying he had a vision of God and heard him calling for a messenger to meet the need, "Whom shall I send, and who will go for us? . . . Here am I," he volunteered, "send me" (Isa. 6:8).

He was eager to obey, whereas many of us hear the pleading for persons to visit, witness, and carry the gospel and say, "Here am I, Lord. Send someone else!"

A pastor or Christian leader who is himself unwilling to face a mission call honestly cannot lead his church to be missionary in its vision. This, like any other area of disobedience, affects his commitment, his prayer life, his ability to preach to and lead others.

Lack of surrender at this point may explain what many mission-minded members have noticed and lament, "Our pastor is so fine, but we never hear anything about missions."

Make it personal:

● Pray for YOUR church to have a burden for a Christless world.

● Pray for YOUR pastor to have a vision of the world's need.

● Pray for God to call someone from YOUR church to serve abroad.

● Pray for others to feel this need of praying "forth" the laborers from YOUR own church.

● Pray for the vocational Christian workers and laymen YOU know personally to face honestly the possibility of God's call to missions.

● Pray for YOURSELF and YOUR family as you relate to his will for his world.

When God has called someone you have helped pray forth, then begins your "long" prayer: the prayer you will pray for that person through all of his preparation for and service on the field.

We will need to pray for him in packing ● moving ● saying good-bye to loved ones ● traveling ● learning a new language ● adjusting to a different culture ● getting accustomed to everyday living conditions, often in a less-developed society ● relating to persons of another culture and language without prejudice and with love ● developing good working relations with fellow missionaries of varying backgrounds, viewpoints and temperament ● coping with problems of health, safety in travel and physical danger ● building a strong family life ● accepting the separation from children away in school, and parents needing support ● acquiring the wisdom to meet overwhelming need with limited resources, time and energy without becoming callous or breaking down ● appropriating God's strength in personal crisis and in times of political and social upheaval ● keeping strong spiritual roots in the Lord without many resources for deepening ● ministering spiritually in an aggressive, yet sensitive way to bring persons to the knowledge of our Lord and Savior, Jesus Christ. All these and many more besides.

Hallesby tells of a furloughing missionary from a country where tropical fevers had weakened and undermined the health of many missionaries. As he bade good-bye to friends in his home community, an elderly, believing woman had clung to his hand, looked him straight in the face and said quietly, "I am going to pray to God for you and ask Him to save you from the fever in order that you may devote all your strength to your work out there."

"And," he added, "I have not felt the fever once during all these years!"[3]

"Look around you! Vast fields of human souls are ripening all around us, and are ready now for reaping. The reapers will be paid good wages and will be gathering eternal souls into the granaries of heaven! What joys await the sower and the reaper, both together!" (John 4:35-36, TLB).

Those of us whose prayers help thrust out the laborers and stand behind them as they work will also share in that joy!

30
Prayer and Those Who Pray

The dear, old gentleman extended a hand gnarled and roughened by years of farming in the West Texas sun and wind. "You don't know me," he remarked self-effacingly. "My name's not important, but I pray for you and your husband."

He kept pulling away as I tried to talk to him. Though I doubt he ever believed me, I would rather have folks like that praying for us than many a "well-known" Christian. His utter integrity, honesty, and simplicity came through. Somehow I feel the Lord listens to his kind.

Who are the ones that pray?

More of them seem to be young, the elderly, the sidelined, the hurt, and the wounded.

Young people pray because they take the Lord simply at his word. "They are willing to give up all for the Lord," believes T. W. Hunt, professor of church music, Southwestern Baptist Theological Seminary, Fort Worth, Texas. "They are still not spoiled by the world."

Old people pray because they have learned what really matters, he adds. "When you get old," explains retired missionary Olive Lawton, "The Lord takes away your strength so you can do what you know is really important. And I just appreciate that so!"

The handicapped, invalids, widows, retired persons, ones who have known great sufferings are the ones Dr. Hunt feels have time to pray and can "catch the spark." "I think they are the ones who are going to take seriously what God wants to take seriously. God seems to like to work with the small people, the poor, the little ones.

"I get excited when I find the hurt and the wounded. The handicapped, the elderly, the ones who have known great sufferings are more likely to be very near the throne. They have been taken there.

"I do not believe for one minute that God is ever the author of illness. But I do not believe God heals everybody. Somehow in the permissive will of God so much of the suffering being experienced in the world is accomplishing things far greater than any other kind of training.

"Jesus said, 'Blessed are the poor in spirit and the ones who mourn.' Why would he stress that if we were not to realize the Christian life contains real grief? I do not believe any difficult

130

circumstances come into our life without the permissive will of God, not his direct desire. He is a father. He loves us. He wants our very best. But he wants our best for eternity.

"The people who have known the greatest difficulties usually know the most about prayer. I watch for them as I speak on prayer in churches around the country. I want these people praying for missions; for workers for the harvest; for the brothers and sisters behind the Iron and Bamboo Curtains. I share with them my burden for the unreached."

Who are the ones who pray?

If most of the prayer warriors are young, past fifty, or the ones wounded in life, as Dr. Hunt believes, what about young and median adults?

"Not everyone falls into the trap," thinks Dr. Hunt, "but many of us experience a time when we feel the world is passing us by and we get caught up in common patterns of turning to the ways of the world in middle years. We want money. We want prestige. We want power. We want success in business, etc. But then the time comes again when we face what really matters . . . especially if we have been deeply hurt."

How have those who pray learned how?

Those I know as serious pray-ers fall generally in four categories.

The first group are those who came from a home with a faithful family altar or a parent who prayed. Whether they have continued the practice faithfully in their own lives or have gotten away from its influence for a period—the basic principles were laid in their lives.

"I learned as a child from my mother's praying and her explanation of prayer," states missionary Jarrett D. Ragan, "that prayer is communion with God, expecting him to answer."

Writes another missionary, "I never heard my parents pray, so naturally I grew up thinking it was not important."

The second type are those who sat under a faithful pastor, teacher, or other church leader who emphasized prayer and prayed with them as individuals or groups.

"I was helped by sentence prayers in our youth Training Union."

"Because I came from a non-Christian home, it was the adult advisers in the various church youth groups that helped me realize the importance of prayer."

"The pastor of our little church really emphasized praying. Finally, he decided to challenge those of us who were really serious about it to attend a 6:30 prayer meeting every morning. For months a small band of us met. I went each day till I moved. Every lost person we prayed for, but one, has come to know the Lord over these years. We are still praying for my father."

Third, there are those who have been "infected" with the desire to pray by a contagious pray-er. Prayer is more caught than taught, as are many things in our faith. It was Jesus' praying that made the disciples want to pray.

"I first became *really* concerned about prayer through the beautiful prayer life of a close friend," explains Doris Bryant.

A group of upperclassmen invited me to a prayer meeting one fall afternoon during my freshman year in college. Sitting by a fence row at the edge to town I listened, learned, and voiced a self-conscious, stumbling prayer. Their concern for fellow students sparked my concern. I had never heard such simple, direct petitions about the spiritual needs and conditions of others. Some of our prayers were judgmental and pharisaical, I'm sure, but the caring was genuine. It sparked a new kind of praying for me, especially when I saw the Lord touch individuals for whom we interceded.

A fourth category of earnest pray-ers is those who have discovered firsthand through experience what every new Christian should be taught: in reality we are helpless and must depend completely on the Lord for everything.

The teaching experience may have been spiritual drought or disillusionment, discouragement or dead-end in ministry, or disappointment, trauma, or crisis personally.

Missionary Sidney L. Goldfinch has learned that "stress drives me to the Lord and thus brings blessing."

"I'm learning that nothing is accomplished without prayer,"

exclaims James M. Tilley. "I tried two years to resolve a problem. When I gave up and washed my hands of it in prayer, the Lord began resolving it in less than two weeks."

Missionary Carolyn Roberson is convinced the Lord put her in an isolated mission station with no other missionaries or Americans near "in order to teach me how to pray."

"When we first became missionaries," recalls Martha Brady, "I resolved, I am going to be a good missionary. I am going to give it all I've got.' And I did! I gave until I collapsed! When I looked back, it wasn't that I couldn't see any results, but I did not see the kind of results I thought there should be. I think the Lord has to bring us to the place of realizing we are nothing."

Analyzing what the Lord has been doing in her life, missionary Glenn Ingouf believes greater dependency on God through prayer may have begun with the illness and death of her ten-year-old daughter, Ann, in 1971. "I just know I am much more aware now of the part that prayer must have if we are to have 'fruit that remains' from any of our work."

Who are the ones who pray for missions and missionaries?

The faithful core are family, personal friends, or those who know the missionaries from previous contact in churches where they worked or have spoken. Former and retired missionaries, missionary-minded pastors, seminary professors, and denominational employees swell the ranks. The backbone of the movement seems to be those involved in missions education organizations who love missionaries and missions. Occasionally there are persons God touches who are committed to him but know nothing about missions, until he touches them with a concern.

Missionary Mary Ellen Dozier knew God was good to deliver her mother from further suffering when he took her, but she missed keenly the loss of her prayers. "No one else prayed for me as she did."

One of missionary Edith Vaughn's first thoughts when her father died was *Who will pray for me now as he did?*

"A longtime Christian friend and my mother-in-law are special prayer warriors for me," says missionary Kay Maroney.

133

A college prayer partner prays for Margaret Robertson, along with an aunt who has encouraged her for years by her interest in all her missionary activities and by assuring her of daily prayers. "She prays daily that six unbelievers will be won to the Lord Jesus."

"Mr. William E. Davidson, former missionary to Chile, started praying for me daily after my praying grandfather died," states missionary Oz Quick.

"When Tom's mother died, we felt a keen loss, knowing she was no longer praying for us," declares another missionary. "On furlough, however, we have found two other ladies who will do this for us."

Expressing it for himself and his colleagues, one missionary feels "it is encouraging to know there are persons concerned enough about our needs and our work to pray for us."

Those of us who pray for missionaries surely were included when Jesus gestured toward his disciples and replied, "There are my mother and brothers! For whoever does the will of my Heavenly Father is brother and sister and mother to me" (Matt. 12:49-50, Phillips).

31
Prayer and Learning

Prayer is a relationship, not a recipe. The Bible sets forth principles to guide prayer, not a set of rules to ensure getting what we wish. There is a world of difference between principles and rules. Principles are broad, basic concepts to be interpreted and applied. Rules are specific, exact regulations to be accepted and followed.

We are guided by principles in our relationship with a personal God. Obeying certain rules about prayer is not an automatic guarantee of specific results. For prayer is relating to a sovereign Lord, not working a foolproof formula. "We will only understand prayer if we start at the beginning—and that means starting with God,"[1] declares Michael Baughen. Most of us are like children, he adds, who feel that we are the center of the world.

Being self-centered is all right, if you're a baby. In fact, it's normal. A baby needs to get acquainted with himself as a starting point for getting acquainted with his world.

It is normal for us as new Christians to be consumed with our new experience. We learn to relate to God as a Father and to ask for our needs. Indeed, we never outgrow that need.

Praying for "our daily bread," as Jesus taught us, should make us conscious that our physical, material needs must be met daily by God. And since we do not live by bread alone, we must also look to him daily for our spiritual nourishment and needs.

A child's self-centeredness, however, should gradually give way to notice of and concern for others. Spiritual "growing up" should mean increasing concern for others and for God's glory, his plan, his purposes, and his ways. "To the degree that we mature spiritually, our prayers will become theocentric, that is, God-centered"[2]

Our prayer life, according to Michael Baughen, must be built on five secure foundations: faith in God as God, and the character of God, the purpose of God, the ways of God, and the promises of God.[3]

Positive Principles for Praying

Listed below are some of the concepts and attitudes needed for relating to God in prayer. It is not an exhaustive list at all, merely a beginning, and will require prayerful study and personal application.

Express praise (Matt. 6:9; Ps. 8:1).

Be thankful (Phil. 4:6; 1 Thess. 5:18).

Acknowledge one's need and dependence on God (2 Chron. 20:12; Prov. 3:5-6; Jer. 9:23-24; John 15:7; 2 Cor. 12:8-10).

Approach with confidence (Heb. 4:16; 1 John 5:14-15).

Repent of specific sin (1 John 1:9; Prov. 28:13; Judg. 10:10).

Confess unforgiveness (Matt. 6:12,14-15).

Ask God to reveal subconscious sin (Ps. 19:12).

Pray for deliverance from temptation and sin (Ps. 19:13; Matt. 6:13).

Come in humility (Jas. 4:6,10).
Be sincere and truthful (Ps. 145:18).
Be specific (Phil. 4:6).
Pray for personal needs (Matt. 6:11; Rom. 15:30-32).
Pray for others' needs (Eph. 3:14-19; Phil. 1:3-4,9-11).
Pray for all men and nations to be saved (1 Tim. 2:1-4; Rom. 10:1; Ps. 67:1-2).
Abide in God's word (John 15:7).
Ask in Jesus' name (John 14:13-14; 16:23-24; 15:16).
Ask for God's glory (John 14:13).
Ask in faith (Matt. 21:22; Mark 11:24).
Pray as the Spirit leads (Eph. 6:18; Jude 20).
Make God's kingdom first priority (Matt. 6:10,33).
Seek God's will (John 7:17; Jas. 1:5; Luke 22:42).
Be submissive to God's will (Judg. 10:15; 2 Cor. 12:8-9).
Be watchful in prayer (Neh. 4:9).
Be alert when praying (Col. 4:2).
Be obedient (1 John 3:22).
Pray at all times (1 Thess. 5:17).
Wait patiently for the Lord (Ps. 40:1).
Persevere in prayer (Luke 18:1).

Often we pray and cannot see, find, or feel an answer. Or we pray and the answer is not what we asked.

It is easier to believe our prayer was not God's will, quit praying, and forget it, than to wait before God and let him show us what is wrong with us or our petition.

When the disciples could not cast out the demon, they asked Jesus, "Why couldn't we do it?" He put his finger on their problem: lack of faith, prayer, and fasting (see Matt. 17:20; Mark 9:29).

The place to go when we fail in prayer is *to* the Lord, not *away* from him. We want to withdraw to avoid his Spirit's probing. If we would learn and grow, we must seek him and his help and counsel, *especially* when we fail.

Facing a very challenging situation, I sought guidance from the

Lord. After a number of weeks of praying and searching the Scriptures, I was given a Bible promise: "Delight thyself also in the Lord; and he shall give thee the desires of thine heart" (Ps. 37:4).

When the project came to a sudden, premature end, I was stunned. The understaking was not that momentous, but I was sure the Lord had promised success in the venture.

It left me shaken spiritually. It was a shock since the Lord seemed to have assured a different outcome. Had the Holy Spirit given me the Bible promise in the first place? Or had I just found it wishfully? (As someone expressed it, had I "grabbed" the verse or had it "grabbed" me?)

For two subsequent years I was in spiritual "limbo" as far as definite guidance was concerned. How could I be sure I was interpreting a Scripture or an impression correctly?

Two years later I related the problem to Tom Elliff whom I heard speak on prayer. Without hesitating, he asked, "Did you delight yourself in the Lord? Or did you delight in A____, B____, or C____?" Immediately I knew the answer as to why my prayer had failed. He had put his finger on my problem. I had delighted in the challenge, not in the Lord.

With most promises there is a condition. If we do not keep the condition, God is not bound to keep the promise. In fact, it would not be good for us if he did.

You can be sure that I have learned to watch for the condition— the "if"—upon which the blessing depends.

Barriers in Praying

The following are other negative concepts and attitudes that hinder our relating properly to God. This listing is only a suggested beginning for personal, in-depth study.

Unbelief (Matt. 13:58; Mark 6:5-6; John 16:8-9).
Unconfessed sin (Ps. 66:18; Isa. 59:1-2).
Unforgiveness (Mark 11:25-26).
Selfish or wrong motives (Jas. 4:3).
Lack of consideration for marital partner (1 Pet. 3:7).
Doubt as to whether you want God's guidance (Jas. 1:5-7).

Idols in the heart (Ezek. 14:7-8).
Lack of action and obedience (Ex. 14:15-16; Jas. 2:17-18).
Unfaithful stewardship of material possessions (Luke 16:11).
Lack of compassion toward poor (Prov. 21:13).
Failure to surrender (John 7:17).
Hypocrisy in worship (Isa. 1:11-15).
Disobedience and rebellion (Jer. 7:16,24).
Ignoring or committing social injustice (Isa. 1:15-17).
Rejecting God's will (1 Sam. 8:18).
Praying to impress people (Matt. 6:5).
Thoughtless, mechanical praying (Matt. 6:7).

Praying is like a skill or an art because it requires training, practice, time, motivation, energy, and concentration.

It is unlike a skill or art in that it does not depend on our ability, as someone has said, but on our availability. The Holy Spirit is ready to teach us whenever we are willing.

"Christ teaches us to pray not only by example, by instruction, by command, by promises," declares Andrew Murray, "but *by showing us* Himself, *the ever-living Intercessor, as our Life*. It is when we believe this, and go and abide in Him for our prayer-life, too, that our fears of not being able to pray aright will vanish, and we shall joyfully and triumphantly trust our Lord to teach us to pray, to be Himself the life and power of our prayer."[4]

The best lesson I ever had as a new missionary about learning a language came after I had finished language school! We had completed a year's formal training, moving on to another city where we were engaged in seminary teaching and church planting. We continued studying several times weekly with tutors who helped us translate material for teaching.

A university English professor, my teacher, was trying to help me translate an illustration into Indonesian. It seemed to me that morning that his suggestions and corrections were too vague and wordy. I wanted an exact translation. So I dropped the story and started on something else.

Very un-Oriental-like, he stopped me. He sensed my feeling that his grasp of English was less than perfect. He was gentle, but pointed.

"Please, Mrs. Parks, may I say this? The difference in you and your husband is this: When you cannot say exactly what you want to say in Indonesian, you stop or switch to English. Your husband, however, 'mem-belok-belok' (meanders). It is the idea of going around and around a winding road. If he cannot say it exactly, he will use what words he knows. He goes around and around the idea until we understand his meaning.

"Let me ask you, Mrs. Parks, are you perfect in your own language?" We laughed, because we both knew the answer, though my father was also a university professor of English. "Well, then," he continued, "you will never be perfect in Indonesian either. But you must keep striving to learn all you can, to be as correct as you can.

"I have taught college English for eighteen years and studied it for ten years before that. I still make many mistakes. I tell my students that the purpose of language is communication. If you can convey your purpose, you have succeeded . . . even if you make mistakes.

"You will keep working to master Indonesian. You want to sound as much like us as you can. Learn our phrases, our inflections, our idioms. Strive for perfection, but use what you know until then."

What a perfect lesson for prayer! We will stop and start, falter and try, fail and succeed at prayer. But as we learn and strive to pray as Jesus commanded us, we will not wait until we are perfect. Learning to pray only comes as we pray.

32
Prayer and Methods

Anyone fearing to "die to self" and follow the Lord lest he lose his personality and his individuality has not become well acquainted with deeply committed Christians. They are as individual as the Lord made their fingerprints.

I have made no extensive survey of devout pray-ers and their methods. But my impression from questioning quite a number leads me to conclude there is no "right way" to pray, if you mean by that a dogmatic, rigid schedule or set of rules. Since God leads us all individually according to our temperament and circumstances, he will lead us individually in our prayer life also.

Richard Elsworth Day, the well-known religious biographer of men who made singular contributions to the cause of Christ, once declared that the one thing they all had in common was they all prayed early in the morning before others arose. I have discovered a few exceptions even to that.

Time is the key.

The factor that keeps recurring as I read about prayer and talk to pray-ers is that prayer takes time. As someone says, "enough time not to be conscious of time." Perhaps the reason older people seem stronger in prayer may be because they have more time. Their children have gone and they are alone more. Time represents interest, commitment, and our very selves. I do not believe we can have a strong prayer life without much time spent in God's Word and meditation.

"God must have for fellowship with himself the first and the best of your time."[1]

The great prayer classics recommend a set devotional time to be guarded zealously. Though prayer is a life-style and the great pray-ers are in prayer and fellowship with God all day long, most agree that without this consistent daily time the all-day-long praying will diminish.

Though most seem to feel that morning is the best "closet" time with the Lord, several will admit that it should be the person's own best time.

One young woman gets up two hours before her family, reads her Bible and studies first, then jogs and prays. Another begins the day by praying her adapted form of the Lord's Prayer each morning, continues praying throughout the day and then has her long devotional time in the evening. One employed homemaker starts at

5:30 AM with a devotional, then uses one coffee break and part of her lunch hour to pray in the company lounge. She carries a notebook containing her prayer list everywhere she goes and snatches moments here and there to pray.

One man who does not consider himself a "morning" person discovered Isaiah 50:4: "The Lord awakens Me morning by morning. He awakens My ear to listen as a disciple" (NASB). "I committed the verse to him, saying, 'Lord, you know I'm a night person and don't wake easily. But I ask you to wake me up because the Lord Jesus prayed in the morning and nearly all the great prayer warriors of history prayed in the morning.' The Lord started waking me up, even though my favorite time to work is still night."

Another person found she had so many responsibilities and activities during one period of her life that she was not having the time for Bible study and prayer she needed. She awoke an hour earlier than usual one morning and lay there worrying about not getting enough sleep, especially since her days were so harried. When this happened several mornings, she realized the Lord was waking her up to pray. Instead of worrying about lost sleep, she decided the Lord knew her needs and began to get up to be with him.

One man prays and concentrates to the end that his first thoughts in the morning and his last ones at night will be of God.

Praying at every opportunity.
One person makes a practice of praying for any person who comes to her mind, since "I do not know any other reason for thinking of them."

Another says she prays for persons she dreams about, feeling this is one way God brings them to her attention.

Instead of just promising to pray for someone, one pray-er stops and prays immediately for the person who requests prayer. "When the need is felt, I pray right then."

A doctor says he has committed himself to pray more with individuals in all situations—at work, home, car, over the phone, and so forth.

Diary of God at work.

More persons seem to be keeping spiritual journals in recent years.

● "I began the principle of keeping a day-by-day intercessory prayer record, making Scripture notations, spiritual insights, and answers. What I have seen God do, been able to record and refer to time and time again, is beyond my broadest 'hope-fors.'"

● "In the last few years I have used a prayer list which has become a sort of prayer journal or diary. I write down as God answers, often including the date. I update or change my method from time to time. I do not know how I survived without it."

● "What I write down includes prayer requests and answers and Bible meditations: in other words, 'What am I saying to God?' and 'What is God saying to me?'"

● "My prayer notebook has two major sections. In the first, I organized my long, long prayer list on a weekly basis, using tab-indexed sections for each day of the week. Now I can pray for everyone and around the world with no hurry. The second section is the daily journal with dates for requests and answers. It has been a great blessing to see how God truly answers day by day."

● A missionary teaches national Christians to keep a written journal. "It is a diary of God at work. It helps them see he lives, to understand more about his personality, and to know he is active in their lives."

A word of caution about listing prayers comes from Gordon Watt: "It is quite possible for Satan to burden us nervously in prayer, creating a feverish anxiety to tabulate answers to our petitions. Let us guard against rush in the prayer life, against the device of the enemy to drive and push us, either to act without prayer, or pray without quietness of spirit."[2]

Intercessors in partnership with missionaries.

Since those who pray are also laborers in the Lord's work, we should pray for the Lord to thrust them out into his harvest just as we pray for missionaries to be called.

142

We need to pray that each missionary will be surrounded by a group of intercessors who feel personally responsible for him or her. As intercessors, we should ask God to assign us the missionaries for whom we should pray.

• Feeling they should do something more specific in helping Christians commit themselves to regular, consistent prayer for missions, missionaries Otis and Martha Brady began to pray the Lord would give them one pray-er in every church where they ministered on furlough.

"It was not done publicly. We would share our idea and announce that anyone feeling they should respond come to us after the service. We tried to give each one a specific person or project to pray for. In every church at least one person responded. There were men, young couples, women—always one in each church. It has been hard to keep up with the correspondence, but we have had many answers to prayer. We really feel this is where the key lies."

• In addition to their annual missionary letter, George and Helen Hardeman began writing a short prayer letter to about five churches who had promised prayer for them. "We included answers to previous requests, one missionary and one national petition with any specific background explanation needed. It has grown to about twenty-five persons and churches and can be put in church bulletins.

"Our major prayer request personally has been that the Lord would call out prayer warriors for us. The response has been amazing."

• "I think back on our earlier newsletters," recalls missionary Indy Whitten. "They were more travel reports or accounts of unusual or funny happenings. Such are good as background but time convinces me that the main thing is to enlist prayer support.

"Formerly I had said repeatedly, 'Pray for us. Pray for the work, etc.' But my concept about the importance and absolute necessity of prayer partners in the States for home and foreign missionaries has changed. A friend impressed on me the need to have definite

143

persons and projects to pray for and to receive reports when the prayers are answered. I began this prayer partnership and many have been the answers as a result of it."

● Wayne Williams and Jim Muse pastored neighboring churches and were students together in seminary. When Jim and his wife, Pat, were appointed missionaries, Williams said to them, "I've not been called to missions, but as long as you serve as missionaries, I promise to pray for you every day and write you a monthly letter."

Twenty-two years later the promise is still being kept. "There were times when the going was so rough we almost despaired," the Muses confess, "but we were always encouraged by remembering Wayne had prayed for us that day and God had heard him.

"There were times we wrote about special needs and he prayed. Only our Heavenly Father really knows all this friend has contributed to our lives through his faithful prayers and cheerful letters."

● After being missionaries twenty years Bob and Jeannie Spear met a lady in Oklahoma who showed them a tattered clipping from the *Baptist Messenger* about their appointment. She had prayed for them every day even though she had never met them.

"There is no way to determine how much physical and spiritual benefit we have received from just this one person, to say nothing of countless others we know and do not know who pray for us.

"There have not been so many dramatic answers as daily strength. Now into our twenty-eighth year, mostly in rural areas, exposed to adverse health conditions, danger on highways, byways, and in lawless areas, we are sure supportive prayer has played a big role in keeping our emotional and spiritual balance in a nonresponsive, radically different culture."

Praying for missionaries you do not know.
● "I pray for ones I do not know like I pray for myself."
● "I pray for the one(s) I do not know like I do for the one(s) I know."
● "I cannot do justice to praying for all on the prayer calendar as I would like, so often I ask the Lord to impress me which one to pray for from the list. As I am quiet before him, he will give me an

144

impression of who to pray for and what to pray for. I then pray for that person all day long."

• "My favorite way to pray in a general way for missionaries is to picture a fountain spring in the mountains with bamboo pipes carrying the water to where it is needed. So I pray, 'Lord, may the missionary be so attached to you, the Fountainhead, through prayer, witnessing, and Bible study, that the waters will flow and the needy people will get what they need. And Lord, prepare hearts for the missionary to touch today."

• "I try to pray in some specific way for each person on the prayer calendar, according to what may be happening in their country if it's in the news, or any specific thing I know."

• "Since I do not know many, I pray for those on the prayer calendar as a group—that they might be encouraged, that they might be in God's will and might continue to feel called."

• "I pray for any I might know personally and then use Philippians 1:9-11 as a pattern for those I do not know."

• "I pray for persons with whom they serve, both nationals and fellow missionaries, and their family members. My prayer is one of seeking to hold them up to the Lord and affirming his purpose for them. I seek to widen the channels of his grace in their lives and in mine by way of renewed commitment and praise for what he will do for and through them."

• "I research each name on the prayer calendar to find out what type work each missionary does, how many other missionaries are in his country, and statistics on the country and Baptist work there. I write the name on a file card and add any information I glean from the mission magazines. I look up each missionary in the photo album and pray for them as I look at their faces. It takes a lot of time and I have thought about cutting back or stopping. But I cannot. Each one needs my prayers."

A pastor pioneers churchwide praying.
Preparing for the Foreign Mission Emphasis, Pastor Rolfe W. Dorsey decided to lead his church in one full week—168 hours—of praying for missions.

"Over and over we have proven our ability to give great sums of money. Perhaps the time has come for great intercession," believes Dorsey. He gathered appropriate Scripture verses, promises, and thanksgivings. Each intercessor was provided a page of model prayers, intercessions, and promises that could be claimed for workers all over the world.

"The vision of power centers (praying churches) all over this planet releasing God's love through intercession for missionaries is awesome. I am filled with wonder at the possibility. During our week of praying in the chapel, the entire missionary force was presented before the throne several times.

"The missionary card file now remains in the prayer chapel, available for every believer who will, to travel to a far part of the globe and stand in intercession with a courageous worker for Jesus.

"Prayer intercessors grow to be like Jesus in the work. Praying, we stand with missionaries on the field, empowering the Word, strengthening the witness, releasing the captive, protecting the worker.

"Jesus waits to empower people who will unite to pray. The aggressive thrust of the gospel to the world can only be enhanced by a praying people."

33
"Lord, Bless the Missionaries"

How does one pray for missionaries?

First, pray realistically.

We can thank God for the missionaries' commitment and dedication and, at the same time, realize that they have their "feet of clay" just as we do. Our admiration and encouragement may *help* them to stay on the mission field, but our realistic prayers can *enable* them to do so.

146

We remove them from the pedestal. "When you idealize a person, you have two problems," declares Jack Gray. "First, you have an unrealistic view of the person. Second, you have an unrealistic view of yourself."

For example, most missionaries are strong-willed. If they were not, they probably would not make it as missionaries. But strong wills can lead to disobedience, as with Moses, or to personal conflicts, as with Paul and Barnabas over John Mark. There is not a person described in the Bible, except Jesus Christ our Savior, who was sinless.

Every sin, large or small, that has ever overtaken other Christians has made "shipwreck" of some missionary. When a moral tragedy, "root of bitterness" (Heb. 12:15), or deep personality conflict has tripped one up, I have mourned, knowing that the missionary was careless in "enemy territory" and some of us did not "hold the ropes" prayerfully as we should have.

When a missionary was forced to withdraw because of serious moral charges, missionary Martha Franks, retired veteran of China and Taiwan, remarked, "Someone did not pray! Either the missionary or someone responsible for him! Or both!"

Missionaries have all the traits we do. They can be prejudiced, ill-tempered, cantankerous, materialistic, lazy, procrastinating, callous, proud, condescending, dictatorial, insensitive, self-centered, petty, consumed with comfort or recreation, irresponsible, you-name-it.

These are not just innocent failings or shortcomings. They are serious sins. Sin destroys the person who sins, damages those around him, and thwarts God's purposes for him and others he should reach with the gospel. At stake are relationships, marriages, and lost people who need God's love.

The writer of Hebrews warns God's people to encourage each other daily lest we have sinful, unbelieving hearts and become hardened into settled rebellion (Heb. 3:12-15). Pray for God to convict the missionary of sin in his life, making him watchful, sensitive, and repentant.

147

Second, Pray specifically for needs you know.

From TV and radio one can be aware if the missionary's country is experiencing any kind of stress—financial, political, social, religious, or natural disaster. From denominational periodicals you may learn of definite personal requests of both missionaries serving in the U.S. and overseas.

Instead of just describing a situation to the Lord, urges Catherine Walker, petition God to do the thing we believe he wants to do. Change a vague, hazy prayer to a definite request.

Third, thank God for answers.

Faith grows by noting and thanking God for answers. If our prayers have objectives, we can recognize the results when they come. Writing them down helps. Thank God for anything you know he has done for, to, or through the missionary—his call, growth, dedication, and service.

Fourth, focus general biblical prayers for specific missionaries.

I must admit that until I began this study I had never really seen the practical value of many biblical prayers that I considered theoretical and intangible, especially in the writings of Paul.

I could subscribe to Paul's asking Christians to pray for healing, for help in trouble, for safe deliverance from unbelievers, for acceptance of him by groups of believers he visited, for God to forgive and save persons from sin, for God to open opportunities to preach the gospel and then, when they came, to enable him to communicate the message clearly and fearlessly. These were "practical" requests, I felt.

But some of his "wordier" prayers seemed ethereal, impractical, and fuzzy to my earthbound mind. Perhaps the Old English translations or my spiritual nearsightedness, or both, clouded my understanding.

I am just beginning to realize what could happen to a twentieth-century missionary if I prayed for him as Paul prayed for the Ephesians:

148

"I pray that out of the glorious richness of his resources he will enable you to know the strength of the Spirit's inner re-inforcement—that Christ may actually live in your hearts by your faith. And I pray that you, rooted and founded in love yourselves, may be able to grasp (with all Christians) how wide and long and deep and high is the love of Christ—and to know for yourselves that love so far above our understanding. So will you be filled through all your being with God himself!" (Eph. 3:16-19, Phillips).

Take a concordance or a topical Bible and look up all references on prayer and intercession. Or, as you read devotionally, mark all of Paul's prayers, benedictions, and personal requests for prayer. Put them in your own words or adapt as written, inserting the missionary's name and praying for him as you pause in your reading.

The following suggested prayers in the New Testament can become a springboard for helping us formulate our own: Ephesians 1:15-19; Philippians 1:9-11; Colossians 1:3-4,9-12; 4:12; 1 Thessalonians 3:12-13; 5:23; 2 Thessalonians 1:11; 2:16-17; Philemon 4-6; Hebrews 13:20-21; 1 Peter 5:10.

Martha Franks suggests an idea used in a meeting she attended where each woman was given a missionary's name. In unison they prayed the Lord's Prayer on behalf of the individual. "Our Father . . . Thy kingdom come, Thy will be done in Missionary So-and-So on earth as it is in heaven . . . Give So-and-So this day his/her daily bread" (based on Matt. 6:9-11).

Lorene Rhodes voices a general prayer daily for missionaries she does not know personally whose names appear on the denominational prayer calendar:

"Father, Lord Jesus, Holy Spirit, bless our missionaries. You know them intimately and by name. You know their needs—all those expressed and many not made known to us. Many are in great physical danger. Their lives are at stake for preaching your Word. Many are discouraged because the progress seems so slow. Many are in lonely places and miss their homeland. Many have their own personal battles to fight against the wiles of the devil. Whatever their needs are, Lord, help them know that you are there and are able to help them meet their needs according to your riches in glory. Bless them real good. I pray in the name of Jesus. Amen."

If we only pray the time-honored "Bless the missionaries today," remembering them on their birthdays, may I suggest we at least broaden it to ask for a good *year* of following and serving the Lord instead of just a good *day!*

34
Now Pray!

The single orchid gracing the Thanksgiving table in tropical Thailand was the largest and most exquisite any of us had ever seen. Missionary Juanita Johnston, an orchid enthusiast and grower, had saved this one for the special occasion.

For more than an hour while we dined in her home in Chonburi, our family and other guests looked at, studied, contemplated, and discussed Juanita's prize flower. We were fascinated with its beauty and learned all we could about orchid-raising.

We had barely left her house to continue our trip when my husband asked if any of us could recall what kind of vase our hostess had used for the centerpiece. None of us could even remember seeing it.

"I noticed," he said, "because I plan to use it for an illustration. It was a simple low glass dish. My point is this: if we are the kind of earthen vessels or containers (2 Cor. 4:7) we ought to be, nobody will even notice us. They will only see Jesus in his glory."

The ministry of intercessory prayer is one of *selflessness* and *love*. We were created to be indwelt by God. To contain his Spirit. To be his co-workers.

God has called all who claim his matchless Son's name to be like him—priests and intercessors for his world. All God needs to ordain us is a helpless, willing, learning heart, and plenty of time.

Missionary Sam James waked at 4 AM New Year's Eve and knew something was wrong. Thieves had cut through the back door of the missionary residence and stolen bicycles and other Christmas gifts, stereo, kitchen equipment, food, etc. James was upset and angry.

Two weeks later they returned and stripped the seminary where the Jameses were assigned. In his anger Sam thought, *We've come 12,000 miles to help you people and you steal us blind!*

During that same period, he ran into hopeless inefficiency and red tape month after month at government offices when he tried to set up a social ministries project.

His frustration mounted to anger as he thought, *I have come to help you people and you are making it impossible for me to serve you and the Lord.*

One Saturday afternoon he was forced to take a cab because his car had broken down. The cab driver, recognizing from his ability in the language that he was no short-term foreigner, said, "You must have been here a long time." Sam replied that he had.

"Then you must like (our) people," declared the driver. Sam sat there thinking, *You are a preacher. You are a Christian. You are a missionary. What are you going to say?*" Finally he said, "Yes, I love (your) people."

The cab driver turned all the way around in his seat, looked me square in the eyes, and asked, 'What do you love about us?' At that particular moment I did not say anything. I did not have anything to say."

It was suppertime when the taxi delivered Sam to his home, but he could not eat. "I had this big lump in my throat. I was defeated. I just went to bed. But I could not sleep."

In the early morning hours he finally got up to think and pray. "I have this conviction that Christianity boiled down to its essence is love—God's kind of love—and I had lost it. It was gone. I said, 'You may as well resign and go home. You are through as a missionary.'

"In my desperation God spoke to me that night. His very words welled up in my heart as I prayed and literally changed my life. He said to me in a very intimate way, 'My son, you are not here because you love these people. You are here because I love them and I want to love them through you.'"

The next morning Sam stopped beside a leper woman, a hideous sight with her nose eaten away and her fingers and feet gone. "I had always turned away before. But I sat down beside her that morning and saw her as God must see her—as a human being worth loving. I told her that Jesus loves her, though she could not respond. She never responded in all the times I told her that, but those may have been the only times in her life that anybody ever told her that."

You and I are like Sam James when God calls us to love and win his world. "When I surrendered to go to the country where God called me, I did not know one person. I did not know the language. I did not know the culture. I did not know the people. How could I say I loved them?

"But God loved them before the foundation of the world, before they were ever created, as he loves all people.

"Our love is too fragile. The only way his love can be communicated is for a person to open his life with its talent, abilities, potential, and promise and allow the Lord to fill his life.

"The only way millions of lost people will know that Jesus loves them is for somebody to listen to the Holy Spirit and say, 'Here am I, send me.'"

And I would add, "Here I am, Lord, love through me. Give through me. Pray through me."

Let us let three missionaries sum it all up:

"God wants most to make me more like him," believes missionary Mildred Cagle. "There is no better way to become like someone than to spend time together. So I must spend more time with the Lord."

Missionary Gary Baldridge has learned from experience: "You can read all the books on prayer, but in the end you have just got to do it."

And missionary Harry Raley adds, "Praying is like picking peas. We just have to get down on our knees and do it."

152

Notes

Foreword

1. Mary E. Farwell, *The Life of William Carey* (Old Tappan, NJ: Fleming H. Revell, 1888), p. 20.

2. From the Revised Standard Version of the Bible, copyrighted 1946, 1952, © 1971, 1973. Subsequent quotations are marked RSV.

3. From *The Amplified Bible*, Old Testament. Copyright © 1962, 1964 by Zondervan Publishing House. Used by permission. Subsequent quotations are marked AMP.

Chapter 1

1. Gordon Watt, *Effectual Fervent Prayer* (Greenville, SC: Great Commission, 1927. Reprinted, 1981), p. 34.

2. Ralph A. Herring, *The Cycle of Prayer* (Nashville: Broadman Press, 1966), pp. 42-43.

3. Ibid., pp. 43-44.

Chapter 3

1. H. Cornell Goerner, *All Nations in God's Purpose* (Nashville: Broadman Press, 1979), pp. 22-23.

2. A. H. Strong, *Miscellanies*, vol. 1 (Philadelphia: The Griffith & Rowland Press, 1912), pp. 217-18.

Chapter 4

1. From the *New American Standard Bible*. Copyright © The Lockman Foundation, 1960, 1962, 1963, 1971, 1972, 1973, 1975. Subsequent quotations are marked NASB.

2. S. D. Gordon, *Quiet Talks on Prayer* (Old Tappan, NJ: Fleming H. Revell, Co., 1904), pp. 53-63.

Chapter 5

1. John Killinger, *Prayer: The Act of Being with God* (Waco: Word Incorporated, 1981), pp. 14-15.

2. This quotation is from the *Good News Bible*, the Bible in Today's English Version. Old Testament: Copyright © American Bible Society 1976; New Testament: Copyright © American Bible Society 1966, 1971, 1976. Used by permission. Subsequent quotations are marked TEV.

3. Rosalind Rinker, *Prayer: Conversing with God* (Grand Rapids: Zondervan Publishing House, 1959), p. 22.

4. G. Campbell Morgan, *The Practice of Prayer* (Grand Rapids: Baker Book House, 1959), p. 15.

5. Verses marked TLB are taken from *The Living Bible*. Copyright © Tyndale House Publishers, Wheaton, IL, 1971. Used by permission. Subsequent quotations are marked TLB.

6. Michael Baughen, *Breaking the Prayer Barrier: Getting Through to God* (Wheaton: Harold Shaw Publishers, 1981), p. 2.

7. Bill Webb, Baptist Press (7-12-82).

Chapter 6

1. Huber Drumwright, "Study on Prayer," Northern Plains Baptist Convention Annual Meeting, 1981 (tape). See *Prayer Discovered*, Broadman Press, 1978, pp. 15-23.

2. Baughen, p. 16.

Chapter 7

1. Bernie May, *Newsletter.* Wycliffe Bible Translators (3-9-81). Morgan, p. 70.

2. Morgan, p. 70.

Chapter 8

1. Baptist Press news release, February 19, 1982.

2. Ibid.

3. J. Edwin Orr, *The Role of Prayer in Spiritual Awakening* (Los Angeles: Oxford Association, 1976), p. 1.

4. Ibid, p. 8.

5. John White, *Daring to Draw Near* (Downers Grove, IL: Inter-Varsity Press, 1977), p. 46.

Chapter 10

1. Maxine Stewart, "Thailand Reports," *The Commission*, Southern Baptist Foreign Missions Journal, April 1979.

Chapter 11

1. Baptist Bulletin, July 22, 1979.

Chapter 13

1. O. Hallesby, *Prayer,* tr. Clarence J. Carlsen (Minneapolis: Augsburg Publishing House, 1931), p. 119.

2. George A. Buttrick, *Prayer* (New York: Abingdon-Cokesbury, 1942), pp. 108 ff.

3. Frank Stagg, *New Testament Theology* (Nashville: Broadman Press, 1962), pp. 281-82.

Chapter 14

1. R. A. Torrey, *How to Pray* (Old Tappan, NJ: Fleming H. Revel Company, 1900), pp. 40-41.

2. George Mueller, *Autobiography*, p. 152.

3. Watt, p. 101.

Chapter 15

1. Andrew Murray, *With Christ in the School of Prayer* (New York: J. H. Sears & Company, Inc., Publishers, n.d.), p. 62.

Chapter 16

1. Andrew Murray, *The Prayer Life* (Chicago: Moody Press, n.d.), p. 133.

2. See Rom. 8:11; 1 Cor. 6:19-20; Gal. 2:20; Eph. 3:14-21; Phil. 1:21; Col. 1:27.

3. Charles Trumbull, *The Life That Wins* (Ft. Washington, PA: Christian Literature Crusade, Inc.), p. 19.

4. Ibid., pp. 20-21.

5. Gordon, p. 186.
6. See Rom. 12:3-8; 1 Cor. 12:7-11; Eph. 4:7,11-13.

Chapter 17
1. W. E. Henley, *Invictus.*
2. Reprinted with permission of Macmillan Publishing Co., Inc. from J. B. Phillips: *The New Testament in Modern English,* Revised Edition. © J. B. Phillips 1958, 1960, 1972. Subsequent quotations are marked Phillips.
3. Murray, *The Prayer Life,* p. 84.
4. Ibid., pp. 29-37.

Chapter 18
1. Torrey, p. 76.
2. Ibid.

Chapter 19
1. From *Weymouth New Testament in Modern Speech* by Richard Francis Weymouth, published by special arrangement with James Clarke and Company, Ltd., and reprinted by permission of Harper and Row, Publishers, Inc.

Chapter 20
1. See Matt. 21:33-34; 24:45-51; 25:14-30.
2. Roger Heidelberg, Baptist Bulletin Service.
3. Murray, *With Christ in the School of Prayer,* p. 130.
4. Ibid., p. 132.
5. Gordon, pp. 10-11.
6. Ibid., p. 18.

Chapter 22
1. Thomas D. Elliff, *Praying for Others* (Nashville: Broadman Press, 1979), p. 12.
2. Killinger, p. 11.
3. Murray, *The Prayer Life,* pp. 17-18.
4. Ibid., p. 19.

Chapter 23
1. Murray, *The Prayer Life,* p. 10.
2. Gordon, pp. 16-17.
3. Elliff, pp. 12-13.
4. Watt, p. 72.
5. John V. Taylor, *The Go-Between God* (New York: SCM Press, 1972), p. 227.
6. Ibid., p. 234.
7. Gordon, pp. 12-13.

Chapter 25
1. Ann is a fictitious name.
2. See Rev. 5:8; 8:3-4.

Chapter 26

1. Ray Summers, *Commentary on Luke* (Waco: Word Publishers, 1972), p. 207.
2. Torrey, pp. 64-65.
3. Ibid, p. 61.
4. Martin R. Smith "How to Develop—and Keep—a Solid Management Team," *Management Review*, American Management Association, p. 45.
5. Ibid.
6. Torrey, p. 66.

Chapter 27

1. From *The New Testament, a Translation in the Language of the People*, by Charles B. Williams. Copyright 1937 and 1966. Moody Press, Moody Bible Institute of Chicago. Used by permission. Subsequent quotations marked Williams.
2. Summers, p. 141.
3. Hallesby, p. 119.
4. Ibid., pp. 19, 21, 24.
5. Murray, *With Christ in the School of Prayer*, p. 49.
6. Gordon, p. 40.

Chapter 28

1. Cecil Ray, "Lifestyle: Friend or Foe of Mission Support," *World Missions Journal*, December 1976, pp. 10-11.
2. Ibid.
3. Torrey, pp. 85-86.
4. Ibid., pp. 86-87.
5. Baptist Press
6. Torrey, p. 87.

Chapter 29

1. E. F. Hallock, *Always in Prayer* (Nashville: Broadman Press, 1966), p. 39.
2. Hallesby, p. 69.
3. Ibid., pp. 67-68.

Chapter 31

1. Baughen, p. 7.
2. White, p. 80.
3. Baughen, Index page.
4. Murray, *With Christ in the School of Prayer*, p. vii.

Chapter 32

1. Murray, *The Prayer Life*, p. 99.
2. Watt, p. 40.